STORIES OF SOUTHERN HUMOR and CRIME: ANTHOLOGY

STORIES OF SOUTHERN HUMOR and CRIME: ANTHOLOGY

Editor: Tom Whitfield
Cover design and interior layout: AngelaDurden.com
Copyright Notices: Some design elements licensed through Corel Corporation's CorelDraw suite of programs. All photos or drawings of authors are supplied by the individuals and belong to them.

Southern Crime
Southern Humor
— ANTHOLOGIES —
BlueRoomBooks.com
Decatur, Georgia

ISBN 13: 978-1-950729-04-3

Table of Contents

THE AUTHORS: HUMOR

Champagne Velvet

Con Chapman

"I heard a story. Don't know if it's true," the campaign manager said as they waited for the returns to come in from the more rural counties. "About Bagley."

"The son?" the advance man, who was younger, asked.

"No, the old man. He was in a tight race. He'd been appointed to the seat when Morris Stark died, so he'd never won it before."

"Who was he up against?"

"Virgil Green. Solid guy. Been mayor of Sedville and people thought he was ready to go higher."

They both looked up at the door where a deliveryman had arrived with several tubs of chicken and sides. "Somebody pay him, would ya?" the campaign manager yelled across the room.

"So what happened?"

"Well, Green was clean, so he had that going for him. 'Clean Green' was what they called him. Even the big papers in the district got behind him. Bagley'd been under suspicion as to how he got water out to his place in Green Ridge. Everybody else had to dig a well; he got pipe laid by the city so he had the only irrigated farm in the county. He said they needed it out his way in case they ever put in sewer, but hell, it'll be a hundred years before that ever happens."

"Must have made his place pretty valuable," said the advance man.

"Sure did. Well, some reporter started nosing around and found out that Bagley and his family had given the mayor a lot of money."

"Nothing wrong with that."

"Yeah, but then he found out some of the workers at his bottling company had given a lot of money too, so he got suspicious."

"How come?"

"They were pretty big checks for guys who drove delivery trucks or worked on a loading dock. So he ran with the story and everybody came to the obvious conclusion."

"What was that?"

The campaign manager looked at the younger man with a quizzical expression, as if to make sure the fellow was serious. "That Bagley'd been writing the checks himself…or reimbursing his workers — with a little something extra."

"Oh. Did they ever prove anything?"

"No. Bagley called all his employees in as soon as he got wind of the story and told them if they knew what was good for them they'd dummy up. And he'd make it worth their while."

"I see," the kid said, but the campaign manager wasn't sure his subordinate had achieved actual political knowledge as opposed to merely correct belief.

"So anyway, Bagley was nowhere near where he needed to be going into the last weekend. As an incumbent he should have been up five, six points. The last poll he took showed it was a dead heat, within the margin of error."

"So what'd he do?"

"Well, it was Candidates Night at the county courthouse in Sedville. All the candidates for office would go up against their opponents, Lincoln-Douglas style."

"How's that work?"

"You flip a coin and the winner decides whether he wants to go first for six minutes, or second for nine —"

"That's not fair."

"I wasn't finished. If you go first you get a three-minute rejoinder, so it's equal."

"That sounds pretty tame."

"It probably would have been, except Bagley knew he was gonna lose. Green was smooth, calm, articulate. Everything Bagley was not."

"What'd he do?"

"His bottling plant was down on Main Street, down beyond where the stores were, so starting to get pretty raggedy. You know that area?"

"No."

"There's always a fair number of bums down there. Guys looking for a next drink. Wondering how the hell they're going to pay for it."

"So?"

"So he rounds up three of them and tells them he's going to buy them a case of beer if they'll do a little job for him. All they have to do is ride around in a car for his campaign. Of course they all said yes."

The advance man snickered at the unfolding plot, although he hadn't figured it out yet.

"Then he asks one of the men who worked for him — a guy nicknamed Zip. Had a gold front tooth that he popped in and out. He asks Zip to go down to the drive-in liquor store and get a case of beer. He can knock off for the night; he wants him to chauffeur these guys around instead."

"Where to?"

"I'm getting to that. So he gives Zip twenty-five dollars. Bagley figures it'll cost a little over twenty and thinks he's being a big spender letting Zip keep the change. Well, Zip wants to make a little money on the deal, so when he gets down to the store he asks what's the cheapest beer you got? And the guy says Champagne Velvet. Sixteen ninety-nine a case. So Zip gets a case of that and drives back to the plant.

"When he gets back, Bagley has four big 'Green for Congress' signs that he ties and tapes to Zip's car and has the three bums get in. He tells Zip to drive them around the town square until they finish the beer or pass out."

The young man laughed out loud now.

"And he tells Zip, 'I'll give you twenty bucks to honk real loud after that guy Green finishes.'"

"So what happened?"

"Just what you'd expect. You got a carful of drunk guys riding in a red convertible T-Bird. Everybody's lookin' at them. Zip's sober so they can't arrest him and can't stop the car. They drive real slow around the town square. Honking and waving to beat the band."

The pollster brought over a bucket of chicken and offered them some. The campaign manager waved him away with a "Not at this hour of the night," but the kid dug in.

"How were the speeches?" the kid asked through a mouthful of chicken.

"Well, Green won the toss and decided to go first. Zip leaned on the horn as they introduced him to polite applause. Everybody turned around to look and the winos started to chant 'Let's go Green! Let's go Green!' Green gave them a sick little smile, then he began."

"What were the issues?"

"The usual. Taxes, national defense, how much pork you could bring back to the district. After he'd finished his six minutes, Green said thanks and Zip's car erupted like it was the second coming. They yelled and screamed and Zip honked the horn, blast after blast. When Green sat down he looked like he'd ate a bad piece of fish."

"And Bagley?"

"Well, he gets up there and waits for the crowd to settle down after a little smattering of applause. Then he starts in real soft-like, saying he represented the good people of the district. The hard-working people. The ones who didn't have time to go gallivanting around, partying on a Sunday night. Then he paused to let it sink in.

"'My opponent,' he says, 'represents everything that's wrong in the direction America's headed. A people dependent on government, who want to take your hard-earned money, the bread off your family's table, to support their indolent lifestyle.'"

"And...did they buy it?"

"They were eating it out of his hand. 'Lifestyle,' he sneered. 'I don't have the time or the money for a lifestyle, and I suspect you don't either. We get up in the morning, put on our work clothes, eat breakfast and go off to our jobs. To make money the old-fashioned way, by hard work. Not a government handout. We don't have lifestyles,' he said. 'We have families. Children! If there's a God in heaven who looks out for the United States of America, we're the future of this great nation, not Mr. Green and his supporters.'"

The kid was silent for a moment, his face a picture of grudging admiration for someone he'd always heard represented the worst in politics: a fat old man with more money than he'd ever be able to spend.

"Did he win?" he asked.

"I think you know the answer. He held that seat for ten years, five more terms. Then he handed it over to his son. The family bought a home in Virginia where they kept horses. He didn't come back here unless it was election time for the most part. Sometimes he'd show up for the State Fair. Sold his business, leased out the farm, had his mail forwarded."

The gall of the stratagem appealed to and repelled the young man at the same time. He let go an emphatic little exhale, a mixture of amusement and contempt.

"So that's politics for you, son," the campaign manager said as he got up to get a soda. "Sooner you figure that out, the better off you'll be."

Con Chapman is a Boston-area writer and author most recently of *Rabbit's Blues: The Life and Music of Johnny Hodges* (Oxford University Press). His work has appeared in The Atlantic, The Boston Globe, The Christian Science Monitor, and a number of literary magazines.

Grandma Made Wine

Ben Kitchens

When I was a wee lad, my maternal grandmother made wine. She made it from blackberries, mulberries, muscadines, and even grapes that she grew in her garden.

When I was a wee lad of eight, I picked blackberries in the dewy mornings of June. And also the mulberries from the old mulberry tree along the path through the woods leading to Grandma's house. I'd sit among the branches of the tree. Eat one mulberry. Put two in my basket.

Together, Grandma and I pressed the juice from the various fruits. Then she'd add cane syrup sugar to the mixture and let it ferment for a few days. While the pressings of the fruits were going on she often talked of the old times.

"How'd you learn how to make wine?" I asked.

"Well, boy, learnt it from my grandpa."

Her grandpa had immigrated here from Wales. He was one of those men who could do most anything. He was a bricklayer and stonemason by trade but could build a house, plant gardens, and was handy with most mechanical things.

While we were doing the pressing, we'd take an occasional break and drink lemonade and eat apple tarts in the shade of an aged pecan tree. Those were good times and I cherish those memories. Her blackberry wine soaked many a fruitcake. If memory serves me right, she would drink a glass of blackberry wine upon retiring to her bed, but not much anytime else.

She read the Bible and her favorite poets — Robert Frost and Robert Burns. I remember her reading me the poem by Robert Burns, "To A Mouse". At the time I was eight and she'd tell me stories from nine to nine-thirty in the evenings. Stories from long ago that had been passed down to her and things she had heard when she was a young girl growing up in Dodge County, Georgia. Then she'd turn out the light.

"It is time to sleep now, son," she'd say.

She never needed an alarm clock for she rose at almost precisely six in the morning while I dozed on. Soon I'd smell the alluring aroma of bacon drifting from her kitchen. She never ate pork but she knew I loved it and soon I'd wipe the sleep from my eyes and go into her kitchen. There would be a big stack of pancakes, scrambled eggs, bacon.

Grandma ate like a bird and drank her hot tea.

"Grandma? Why do you eat so little?" I'd ask.

She'd smile her little smile. "I was taught womenfolk should not eat like pigs as men do."

I'd ponder her answer and dive back into the syrup-soaked pancakes with fresh butter drizzling down the sides.

As I grew older I often spent the night with her. I no longer slept with her but would lay on the pull-out sofa, reading books and comic books until I fell asleep. One night I decided to go into the pantry and taste her wine. I poured a big glass of it and drank it down. After a few minutes I began to feel a little woozy so I drifted off to sleep and slept a most peaceful slumber filled with wonderful dreams. All at once I felt her gentle touch on my shoulder.

"Did you get into my wine last night?"

"Yes ma'am," I sleepily replied.

"Well, boy, ye are too young to drink wine. Wait until ye are a full-grown man and even then drink it in moderation as Jesus Christ did."

"Yes ma'am."

"Now get on up, son. I got your breakfast ready for ye."

I slowly walked into her kitchen and there before me was her big stack of pancakes, scrambled eggs, and bacon. She often made jelly and jam from different fruits. Sometimes I preferred to eat the pancakes with grape jelly. For some reason that morning I had a dull headache and didn't have much of an appetite. But she had prepared a table before me and so I forced myself and partook of it.

As the years rolled on I became a surly teenager, confident in the superiority of my own knowledge. I was far wiser and smarter than Grandma and now very seldom slept over at her house. I'd visit occasionally but paid little attention to her wisdom. Still, one thing always stood out in her wise teachings. She taught me, or should I say instilled in me, never to be quick to anger.

One day she said to me, "I want to tell you something."

I was eager to leave and wander in the woods but stayed and listened to her words. She told me of her late husband who had passed away twenty four days before I was born. "Your grandfather had a quick temper and when he would drink too much wine or whiskey it would be even worse."

I listened.

"If ye get angry at petty things it will cause your blood pressure to rise. If your blood pressure rises frequently then you will develop chronic high blood pressure."

She went on to explain exactly what high blood pressure meant. Still I listened and she went on in her soft, Southern accent.

"He'd get mad at the drop of a hat. So, one day in 1947, he became very angry at a man in a store. He got so angry that he had a stroke that rendered him partially paralyzed."

"Why did he get so angry?" I asked her.

Shaking her head, teardrops slowly coming from her blue eyes, she said, "I never knew why he was ruled by his anger. If only he had just drank a little glass of wine each night he probably would not have been that way. Now mind you, he was not a drunkard; but he had bitterness inside of him from what he said his family had done to him."

I listened on.

"Do you remember years ago when you drank my wine?"

I nodded.

"Well, some people have a natural-born tendency to become angry, but when they drink too much wine or whiskey they become even more angry. That is why I said to you 'Do not drink until you are a full-grown man and even then drink to moderation as Jesus Christ did.' Do everything in moderation."

While she was talking I noticed a mouse slowly moving across her kitchen.

"Grandma! There's a mouse in your kitchen and it's coming out of your pantry."

She chuckled and said, "Well, I guess that wee mouse has done found its way into my wine."

"You reckon it's gonna get mad, Grandma?"

She chuckled again and quoted a line from a Robert Burns poem. "Sometimes the well-laid plans of mice and men often go awry."

"What does that mean, Grandma?" I asked.

"Well, I think that wee mousie was a-planning to get into my cheese but because of the wine I had sitting in a bowl his plans didn't quite work out."

We had a good laugh.

"Do you want me to kill it?" I offered.

"No, my boy. Let it go its way. All God's creatures have to go their own way."

- - - - - -

Ben Kitchens is shy.

High Flying Jets

A. Shane Etter

I am a son of the South. Born and raised in Jackson, Mississippi. As such, of course, that meant watching Ole Miss or Mississippi State on beautiful autumn Saturday afternoons. But somehow I was drawn to professional football on Sundays. A simpler time. Where black shoes ruled, hair was cut high and tight, and professional football players wore white shirts and ties under plaid jackets and sometimes over plaid slacks. This was before Monday Night Football became the media event not to be missed.

In my teens, Joe Willie Namath captured my attention. "Broadway Joe" brought style and panache to the rough-and-tumble world of sports. Long hair and his trademark white shoes. Wooing movie stars. Responsible for making pantyhose fly from shelves when he posed in a pair. Sex symbol. Hound dog. Guest star. Movie star. Icon.

I was not the only male, teenage or otherwise, who aimed to emulate his walk, his slouch, and his savoir faire. Hell, Joe was the inventor of cool. But I perfected it. And a half century later I'm still cool. Just ask anyone who knows me. They will tell you so, or at least tell you I think so.

But years later it would be me that would warn Joe about minding his manners. And it would be me who saved the Jets one afternoon in a hotel in the Crescent City.

Here's how that came to be.

After a couple of years of never missing Jets games on TV, those years wrapped around their Super Bowl III win on January 12, 1969 — Joe's number, by the way, twelve. There was this one time I broke up with a girlfriend when she phoned me during a game because she just wanted to see if she could get me away from the TV. That's when I began having a recurring dream that the Jets played a game in my hometown, Jackson, at the stadium where Ole Miss and Mississippi State played a couple of games a year to placate their capital city fans. Alas, in the light of day I knew that would never happen since Jackson didn't have an NFL team.

Eventually, once a little older and able to make decisions for myself — and now married — I decided I should go to some Jets games. After twenty years of following Joe and the Jets, the Jets were going play the Saints in New Orleans.

This was long before the day of terrorism and other evil events, so I called up the Jets.

To this Southerner's ears the cultured voice of a lady from New York answering their phone sounded harsh. I told her I was a lifelong fan and asked in which hotel the team would be staying in the Crescent City.

You laugh because now you would never get that information. But believe it or not, she told me. And thus armed, with Jackson in my rearview mirror, I drove south toward New Orleans on a chilly Saturday morning in November with hopes of meeting my newest generation of Jets heroes. When the Jets bus pulled up in front of the hotel's entrance and players I recognized strolled in, well, I was thirteen all over again. I became the kid who loved Joe Namath, the Jets, and every future player that would ever wear the Kelly green and white. (Years later the color would morph to a darker shade that some NFL marketing genius deemed *forest* green.)

In any case, I met and got pictures with several of the more famous players I had been watching. Each was kind and accommodating.

But the most fortuitous meeting was with a man not much younger than me, their Vice President of Operations. He offered his hand and name. When he found out that I, who was only in my mid-thirties, had more than a twenty-year legacy of Jets loyalty, he handed me his business card with the iconic green Jets logo and told me to keep in touch. Anytime I wanted to go to a game, he said, I was to let him know and he would tell me the hotel in which they would be staying and he'd get me tickets to the game.

Jackpot!

He did what he said he would. Thereafter, at the beginning of every season for many years, when schedules were announced, I'd email him with a list of the games my wife and I wanted to attend. Back would come the hotels in the away cities. By then I knew the hotel where they stayed in New Jersey for home games. After quite a few Jets games and having game tickets hand-delivered to us at the team hotel, the Jets finally did what I had always wished for —

They played preseason games on two consecutive summers in my hometown. My wish had come true. By this time, however, we had moved to Atlanta. A road trip to my thirteen-year-old self followed.

We still had family in Jackson. But much to their chagrin, as was our habit at Jets games, we checked into the team's hotel on Capitol Street. It was a half block west of the antebellum governor's mansion where I had attended soirées when I had dated a previous governor's youngest daughter.

The Jets were the home team in Jackson, Mississippi, in a game against the Philadelphia Iggles, as the Philly fans called their Eagles. Two teams from cities ninety four miles apart traveled a thousand miles to play each other.

Having met the greatest Jet of all time a couple of years before, imagine my surprise when I returned to the lobby from our room to find Joe Namath putting the moves on my wife.

Joe looked up, embarrassment coloring his face red. "Shane, how you doin'?" he said in his famously sexy drawl.

Having a black belt in karate, I could kick Joe's ass and he knew it. But I didn't want to do that. So, calmly but quite firmly, I delivered a lesson in manners toward my wife.

"Joe. You wouldn't want me to hurt you."

I stared at him. I did not smile. He shuffled off in his trademark shoulder slump — lesson learned.

Over the next fifteen years or so, we traveled the country going to close to a hundred Jets games, meeting and even becoming friends with many of their biggest stars like Keyshawn Johnson, Curtis Martin, and Wayne Chrebet.

Once again they went to New Orleans to do battle with the Saints in a Sunday night prime-time nationally televised game. With seven hours until kickoff, the team's equipment guys left for the Superdome in a panel truck loaded with uniforms, equipment, and footballs. Still at the hotel, the head coach decided he wanted the team to have a walk-through practice in the parking deck. Alas, their footballs were in the panel truck on their way to the stadium.

Kevin Mawae, the Pro Bowl center who snaps the ball on every play, told me about their predicament. I said, "I have a ball in my room."

I always had a football with me on game weekends. Hey, you never know when autograph opportunities will arise, right? So, I ran through the lobby to my room and back, much like a certain one of my heroes, football cradled securely in hand, to be met by slow rhythmic applause of the players and shouts of "All right! Shane's got a football." Even though Joe Namath had hit on my wife a few years before, I magnanimously didn't hold it against my team.

You might not believe this story. You may believe it to be fiction. But it is true: I loaned the New York Jets my football so they could hold a game-day practice. But, before they returned the football to me, Jets quarterback Vinny Testaverde and wide receiver Wayne Chrebet signed it.

I loaned the Jets a football and got back a treasure.

A. Shane Etter is a former high tech sales professional who started writing fiction to improve his brain after suffering a stroke.

He has seven published novels. His first novel, *Bottom Dwellers*, was named the best murder mystery of 2012 by the late publicist/agent/author John Weaver. *A Brain In Third Person* was named by Amazon Top 300 reviewer Cyrus Webb as one of his twenty five favorite novels of 2018.

Shane was born, raised, and educated in the literary state of Mississippi and has called greater Atlanta home for almost 30 years.

Disney on the Cheap

William Steven Farmer

Summer, 1983. And my wife got it in her head that we just had to see Disney World.

"It's Mickey," she said, a bit of longing and expectation in her voice. "They opened that new 'EPCOT' thingy. How can you *not* want to go?"

We were working adults who would have to take at least one day off work, had little money, and no kids for crying out loud, but that reality didn't make a dent in her logic.

"Kids?" she said. "If it's kids you want, let's ask your brother to go. He's got a brand-new one." The kid wasn't eight months old yet.

But Wife had made up her mind. Things weren't going my way. I could hear the beat of an old, random rock song building in my brain. It sounds strange but it helps me cope with stress. Sighing, I left the room to "Chantilly Lace".

Before I knew it, she invited my brother, his wife, and their new baby. Now we were going with a baby. Great. The kid, her mother's princess, was okay, but the idea of tromping around Disney with a screaming, crying bundle of joy wasn't what I had in mind. It wasn't what my brother and his wife had in mind either, but my loving wife had told them that I would be ecstatic to help.

"Charlie Brown" released stress that time.

Three days before we were scheduled to leave, my brother called to let me know, out of courtesy, that he had invited our parents to join us. Where would this vacation disaster end? My car wasn't big enough. His car wasn't big enough. But, he assured, he would work something out.

Come departure day, Saturday morning, we headed south from Atlanta in a conversion van he borrowed from his brother-in-law who ran a used car lot. I had to hand it to him. The van was a nice touch. It had cruise control. What a great idea. Heading down I-75, I set that sucker just south of Morrow and didn't touch a pedal until we crossed the Florida line. That has to be some kind of record. I had to get me one of those. As the miles drifted by it became obvious that I was the designated driver. This wasn't a problem for me. My brother's driving reminded me of a race amongst the turtles; my father, who rather enjoyed being about eight feet from the other guy's bumper, scared me to death.

After filling the tank in Lake City, the three of us stood beside the pump for a few seconds in silence. As the awkwardness grew, I realized they weren't going to help with the gas. I had been here before. It occurred to me that borrowing the van was my brother's idea of sharing the load and Dad was between jobs. I finally stepped inside the store. The harmony of the Beach Boys playing in the background calmed me as I realized my shrinking wallet might not go the distance.

We arrived in Kissimmee and found our rooms without a problem. No Disney-themed hotel for us. Our chain motel was the largest I'd ever seen. Just a mile or so outside the park, it consisted of five four-story buildings, over nine hundred rooms, and a large office/restaurant complex.

Back home my mother worked as a cook for a branch of that hotel and had arranged for two rooms; one for my brother, his wife, and baby, and one for the rest of us. A room with my Mom and Dad wasn't my idea either, but my loving wife had explained that it was the only way they could afford to go. She said it with an air of superiority, as if she thought my wallet was a home for wayward hundred-dollar bills.

Upon check-in, my brother, who didn't have a nickel to his name, brandished a new credit card. "It's my brother-in-law's," he chuckled and shook his head as he took his keys and returned to the van. The situation could have been worse. We could have stood around looking at each other until I broke down again but, this time at least, he paid for his own room.

With no card of my own, I was left paying cash. "Three nights, four adults, one room, just like it says on the reservation," I muttered as I fished the money from my wallet. Mister Anthony Carter, Desk Manager, a very officious looking man, glared at me over his glasses and demanded my driver's license before handing over the keys. A chorus or two of "Summer in the City" and the realization that I probably wouldn't have to deal with him again calmed me as I moved to the door.

Our rooms were on the top floor in the rear of the fifth building. These buildings, common for the time, had stairs and walkways on the exterior and no elevators. We schlepped luggage all the way to the fourth floor and collapsed through the door.

Our room was around 100 degrees in the Florida heat, so we decided to get a bite while it cooled down. We descended the stairway like dejected Himalayan sherpas and as I turned toward the restaurant, Mom grabbed my arm.

"I don't want to eat here," she said, scowling. "I get enough of their excuse-for-food at home."

Did I mention she was the cook for one of the motel's Atlanta locations?

On the way to find what might or might not be a better choice, my brother's wife mentioned their room felt like a cooler. My brother was always the lucky one and everyone knew it. I caught Dad's eye and we just shook our heads in resignation. Later, back at the rooms, everyone had a shower and settled in. It had been a long day. I was looking forward to a good night's sleep.

Silly me.

Exactly at 1:15 AM, someone tried to open our door. The chain held. But Mister Joe Fielding from Kansas City, Kansas, cursed under his breath. He had carried luggage up four flights of stairs to find the room he'd been given was already occupied.

I threw on some clothes and, after a brief conversation, we called the front desk. Mister Anthony Carter, Desk Manager, had no record of assigning the room to me. He demanded I come down to the office to "explain my presence". Oh, I was more than ready to explain my presence in great detail so, accompanied by Mister Joe Fielding, from Kansas City, Kansas, and his luggage, I led our angry two-man parade to the office posthaste.

Mister Anthony Carter, Desk Manager, met me with a scowl. "I don't know how you got in our room sir, but I assure you, we won't hesitate to have you removed by the proper authorities."

"I got in your room by paying for it. Cash!" I said with venom dripping from my clinched jaws. "Here's my receipt." Amazingly enough, I had kept it. Mister Joe Fielding, from Kansas City, Kansas, took a step back and looked around the lobby before grinning ear to ear.

Confirming I had, indeed, paid in advance for three nights, Mister Anthony Carter, Desk Manager, harrumphed a faint apology and found for Mister Joe Fielding from Kansas City, Kansas, another room just down the walkway from us. I helped him back up Mount Kilauea with his luggage and finally got to bed around 2:30. Sleep didn't come easy.

I went through most of the 1964 hit parade before slipping under its magic spell.

The next morning, tired but showered and shaved and looking for a fun time in the park, we left the room. Mom and Dad walked down with Brother's family, laughing all the way. Getting no sympathy from my wife about the lost sleep, I suggested the restaurant at the inn might be okay for breakfast but was deterred by Mother again. Calling up from the walkway below she pleaded, "No motel food. And don't go to that place you took us to last night. It was nasty!"

I found a pancake house near the entrance to the park and pulled in. Brother, the one with the credit card, complained about the prices but ordered extra. I thought the pancakes were superb and inexpensive too. We ate our fill and headed to the park.

We found parking under a huge painted likeness of Goofy, evidently put there to help us find our way back to the borrowed van. We could see other figures scattered throughout the vast expanse of asphalt desert. About eight feet high, these colorful cartoon figures, mounted on tall poles, presided over thousands of their charges for the day: Fords and Chevys.

Almost immediately a tram stopped a short distance away. Three cars long with seating down both sides and pulled by a small tractor, it could hold about fifty people. We almost didn't get aboard in the rush of pseudo-Mouseketeers but were able to claim enough room for us, the cameras, bags, hats, and baby paraphernalia.

The ride over to the monorail station was uneventful. Quickly boarding the futuristic train, we gazed at the large topiary characters along the tracks. Then, as the crowd gasped, it passed through a huge hotel. Imagine riding a train through the towering atrium of a futuristic A-shaped building at about thirty miles an hour while people point and wave as you go by.

Surreal!

Then it was time to pay. Brother pulled out the magic credit card and quickly bought his tickets. Did that sucker not have a limit? Was his brother-in-law independently wealthy? Insane? Brother smiled smugly as he led his wife through the turnstiles. By now I wondered just who was going to pay that bill: Him or the brother-in-law?

Dad slipped me a twenty to cover their tickets. I was going to point out the pricing chart but was intercepted by my wife who nudged me to the line frowning, "Be nice." I dug deeper in my wallet while the girl at the ticket window waited. My wallet was shrinking by the minute. I sighed and bought four tickets.

The Righteous Brothers were clearing their throats and…

…that's when I was handed Princess for the first time. Evidently the backpack I bought, built specifically to carry infants, was unacceptable. Princess was adamant on that point. I spent the better part of our first day carrying the backpack on my back — and Princess on my hip.

The Magic Kingdom at Disney World is amazing. Shows, rides, the spectacle that is Disney completely engulf the visitor. I would have liked to fully experience all of its pleasures but, alas, I had the baby. Everyone was having a great time — save the baby and myself. Princess began to hit her stride, though, after waking from a sound sleep in Pirates of the Caribbean. Huge grins in the Tiki Tiki Room, then full-on giggles. Just a small silver lining to the cloud that was my chore — and the baby wasn't even mine.

Looking around, I imagined what we could have done without a baby and family tagging along. I thought about the cost and trouble of getting to where we were and, as everyone else enjoyed the park, I sat with Princess and listened to the increasing strains of "Stand By Me" float from my subconscious.

Dad, at first observing without comment the grandeur that was The Magic Kingdom, began to warm to the experience. Walking out of the Tiki Tiki Room he grinned and said, "Son, if I had that place in Blue Ridge, I'd make a fortune!"

While my brother and our wives rode Space Mountain, I sat with Mom and Dad sipping an ice water and trying to keep Princess amused. It wasn't easy. You would think that sitting in an amusement park with life-sized cartoon characters at every turn would, at least, get her attention.

You would be wrong.

Alternately squirming, crying, and bouncing in my lap as she pulled my ears seemed to be her sole purpose in life. It was the baby or me. A challenge if you will. I had made my mind up that she wasn't going to beat me.

Silly me.

I carried her around on my shoulders.

I waved her in front of Mickey, Pluto, Daisy, Goofy, even a chorus line from the "Silly Symphonies" with no effect.

She finally fell asleep and then, in an attempt to get some relief, I asked my mother to help me move her into the baby carrier on my back. This lasted all of ten seconds. I knew she was awake when she grabbed a handful of my hair, pulled herself upright, and bellowed for reinforcements in her struggle to defeat her dear uncle.

Bless her, Mom offered to help but by that time it was too late. I had lost and we all knew it. My only salvation was the brain-pounding chorus to "Summer in the City" brought to life by her incessant tugs of scalp grass.

Before dark, Dad was ready to get out of the park. "Son, there are a lot of people in this place. I don't want to get to the motel after midnight."

"Disney knows how to run the place," I told him as I swapped the kid to the other hip for the umpteenth time. "We'll be okay." I didn't have a clue, but I did have an ulterior motive.

I wanted to catch the Main Street Parade.

Friends back home had assured that, along with the following fireworks over the lake, the parade was not to be missed.

What a spectacle. Music blared from every enormous float, each depicting a scene from a different movie. Pinocchio, Dumbo, and Tinkerbell were chased by Captain Hook and his croc, Tick-Tock. The crocodile was moonlighting from his regular gig down the road in the Everglades.

Everyone enjoyed the parade. At least the baby and I did. She pounded the beat of the music on my ear as she bounced and squalled with delight. I was having such a good time I didn't care.

In the meantime, Dad kept mumbling about moving closer to the exit while looking around and shaking his head. I assured him repeatedly that it would be okay. I wasn't going to leave when I was finally having a good time. After the fireworks — they were as magnificent as had been reported — we hit the monorail and tram and were back to our van in less than 15 minutes. Loading into the van, Dad, a veteran of Korea, looked around and said with a sheepish grin, "The Army could take a few lessons from this place in moving troops." We had a good laugh and headed back to the motel.

After spending the whole day at Disney lugging around a kid that wasn't mine, I wanted a shower and soft bed. What I didn't want was to find the room untouched at 10:30 PM. No beds made? No fresh towels? I called the front desk and Mister Anthony Carter, Desk Manager, answered. He assured me he had the best housekeeping staff in the business and someone would be by soon.

At 11:30 Mom said, "That's it. Come on." She stormed out the door, ready for a shower herself. Knowing her way around the chain's inner workings, Mom quickly found a supply closet. We loaded up on towels and washcloths. While we were gone, my wife made the beds and we finally settled in sometime around 1 AM.

Two hours later a knock came at the door. "Not again," I mumbled to myself, but it was only a security guard who handed me towels and washcloths. Without a word or a smile he turned and left. I threw them into the bathroom, shaking my head in frustration, and fell back into bed.

At exactly 3:16 AM, though, Mister Billy Crabb of Memphis, Tennessee, accompanied by his wife and two children, opened the door. I was sensing a pattern. The chain held again, and again I heard a few choice words slip through the opening. After explaining the situation I called the front desk. The ever-present Mister Anthony Carter, Desk

Manager, surprisingly could not remember the previous night, and demanded a face-to-face again.

After a quick discussion about luggage and how I had to help carry the bags of Mister Joe Fielding from Kansas City, Kansas, back up the night before, Mister Billy Crabb of Memphis, Tennessee, agreed to leave their five bags in our room while we sorted out the problem. The wife and children went back to their car to wait it out. A smart move as Wife and Mother were mad enough to spit nails. Dad slept through it all, a smile on his tired face.

At the desk I again confronted good ol' Mister Anthony Carter, Desk Manager. He still did not remember me and, evidently, had removed the confusion of the previous night from his meager brain to make room for more pressing pursuits. I reminded him, slowly, and in great detail, of our previous conversation. While displaying my receipt again, I felt I was in control of body, mind, and emotions.

You may disagree.

"Because I enjoy our nocturnal conversations so much," I continued, a quiver in my voice, "let me also inform you that, for my money, 'the best housekeeping staff in the business' sucks!"

Mister Anthony Carter, Desk Manager, was quite apologetic this time and assured me everything would be taken care of. He also assigned Mister Billy Crabb of Memphis, Tennessee, along with his wife and two children, a room on the top floor of the first building. I thought it only right to help him with his luggage, not a small journey as it turned out. I was able to fall back in bed around 5 AM. Sleep did not come.

I found, to my chagrin, one can't sleep while Led Zeppelin pounds in the back of the brain.

On the way out the next morning I saw a large grey suitcase, apparently abandoned, sitting on the third-floor landing. I assumed someone was loading up and would be back up to get it soon so continued on.

Once in the van it was agreed breakfast in the local places was too expensive. Evidently, the magic credit card wasn't as magic as I thought. This was against my better judgment. It was my opinion that food, outside the park at least, was the one thing we could afford. After all, you had to have it.

After a stop at the Quick Shop, we devoured a hearty meal of bologna and Wonder Bread with just a hint of mustard as a side. This feast was completed with a splash of cola. My wife finished off the shared can as we parked under Pluto.

Tram. Monorail. Tickets. Finally we were inside EPCOT. As we gazed at the marvel that is Spaceship Earth, they gave me the baby again.

Oh, joy.

The new park was amazing. Dad and Brother loved The World of Tomorrow, as did Mother and the wives. Princess spent the entire time crawling up her own adventure ride — Mount Cranium — while I tried to ignore her. One of these days I'm going back to see what they found so amusing.

The assorted country pavilions, arranged around a pristine lake, were interesting, but the main attraction, in my mind at least, was the Hall of Presidents display. Each American president throughout history was represented by his own audio-animatronics figure. They all moved and some spoke. Princess answered every one of them loudly, insistently, and right in my ear.

We got back to the motel, dead tired, about 8 PM. The suitcase, untouched by owner, employee, or thief, was still there so, as everyone else went on up to our rooms, I took it to the front desk.

"Oh, Lord," gushed my front desk friend, Mister Anthony Carter, Desk Manager. "Where did you find that? We've been hunting it all day. The owners have called almost every hour in a panic."

I smiled to myself knowing that good ol' Mister Anthony Carter, Desk Manager, didn't have that kind of memory.

I explained where it had been, while wondering how on earth they could have missed it sitting in the open. Then I realized anew who I was dealing with. He shook my hand and thanked me profusely. He even asked my name and room number. What a genius our Mister Anthony Carter, Desk Manager, was. I didn't think I needed to repeat it, it wouldn't take anyway, but by that time I was too tired to care.

Back in the room the situation hadn't changed; beds still unmade and no new towels. But luckily, we still had the ones the guard delivered the night before. I was going to complain again but Mother stopped me.

"Do you really want the guard showing up at 1 AM again to make the beds?"

She had a point.

We made do and were in bed by 11. Finally, a chance to sleep, perchance to dream. At 1:37 AM the door opened. Mister and Mrs. Philip Corrigan of Sioux City, Iowa, were stopped by the overworked chain. Curses ensued from both sides of the door. My pattern theory confirmed, I took a minute to explain the situation to them. This was a speech I now knew by heart, and I told them I had made up my mind and I wasn't leaving the room this time.

I called the front desk, identified myself, and gave my room number. My bosom buddy, Mister Anthony Carter, Desk Manager, after a brief pause, assured me I was wrong. That room was assigned to another guest and would I please recheck. The number was, conveniently, right there on the front of the phone. I took a very deep breath, began tapping my finger to the beat of an old Platters number and began recounting previous meetings.

Within a few seconds he stopped me with an, "Oh my! Is this who I think it is?"

I slammed the phone back in its cradle and turned back to the Corrigans. "The desk will assign you a new room. Please speak slowly to my friend Mister Anthony Carter, Desk Manager, and for God's sake, keep a receipt."

The next morning I'd had enough of the whole situation. Ignoring my now-depleted wallet, I pulled my emergency funds from my sock and paid for everyone's excellent breakfast in the inn's restaurant. Mom had bacon and eggs and then, with a faint smile, quietly ordered pancakes.

My brother and I loaded the van for the return trip. We were standing in the warming sun, waiting for the others to descend the stairs one last time, when he turned to me and said, "This motel was a great find. I've got to hand it to Mom. The assistant manager, a very nice man named Carter, stopped by our room this morning. Imagine that. In a place this big. He said he was sorry for all the trouble. I told him we hadn't had any trouble. Our room was just fine the whole stay. You know, he insisted on giving me a voucher for a three-night stay anywhere in the U.S. I think I'll use it next month to take Meg and the baby to the beach."

I was so frustrated I couldn't even think of a song to distract myself. After a few seconds to let the frustration pass, I smiled and asked, "Brother, I'm tapped out. Do you think there's enough left on that card to cover gas on the way home? Since you're driving, I'm sure it will be convenient."

I planted myself in the rear of the van, closed my eyes, and fell into a Simon and Garfunkel daze.

Nine hours later we fell through the front door of our apartment; penniless, Disney engorged, and glad to be home.

That's when my wife piped up. "Honey? I've heard Gatlinburg in the fall is very nice. Do you think your family would be interested?"

HENDRIX!

William Steven Farmer, a true jack of all trades and master of none, is a retired fire department Battalion Chief, and now a real estate investor living in McDonough, Georgia. He also plays harp guitar and writes songs. The first thing Steve wrote got published in The Reader's Digest. He is now three-for-three.

facebook.com/steve.farmer.330

Kitty Doolittle, Stay-at-Home P.I.

Jennifer Milne

1.

I wasn't sure which was worse: The knitting needle pressed against my throat or the gun with the handmade rainbow yarn koozie around its barrel pointed straight at my chest.

"Last chance, sugar," warned the sweet little old lady who was threatening to murder me.

"I don't have it," I said roughly.

"Stop lying to us, young lady," said the other sweet little old lady who held the gun on me. She wore a sweater with sweater-wearing poodles on it. It was very meta.

"I. Don't. Have. It," I said again as the cold tip of the needle pressed harder against my skin.

"Then I'm going to have to kill you, dear," said poodle-sweater lady, as she leveled the gun at my chest.

It's funny what you think about as you're about to die. People usually say they see their life flash before their eyes. Or they remember every mistake. Or are suddenly filled with regrets.

Not me, though.

All I could think about was my casserole.

2.

TWO DAYS EARLIER

"You don't look like the type of person who would do this kind of work," said my client, as we sat in the rent-by-the-hour motel room by the airport.

"You know, I get that a lot," I said jovially, as I dug through my bag.

"Uh…are those kittens on your purse?" he asked me.

"They're uni-kitties—a mix of kittens and unicorns. And it's a diaper bag, not a purse. My kids aren't in diapers anymore but you can't beat a diaper bag for size and durability."

"Oh, that's…nice. Um, so how did you end up doing this? Wouldn't one of those at-home sales jobs be more…appropriate?" he asked, obviously trying to mask his discomfort with our situation.

"Well, the oils gave me hives. I have no use for a pink convertible. And you can only talk with excitement about an airtight food storage container once…maybe twice. No, I stand by once."

"My wife sells those weight-loss shakes," he said, then flinched. "Sorry, I probably shouldn't talk about...uh..."

"No, it's all right," I assured him. Talking with the client and making them feel comfortable was just as important as the work itself. "Now," I said, as I finished setting up. "Just a reminder, I only deal with cash."

He nodded. "Of course."

"Great, so why don't you tell me why you want me to investigate your mother?"

* * * * *

"I'll be home soon, Honey," I said into my cellphone to my husband. "The PTA meeting ran a little longer than I thought it would....There's a lasagna in the fridge....Just pop it in the oven for twenty....Please make sure the kids all get their homework done, and I'll be there in a jif. Okay?... Love you too. Bye."

I hung up the phone and sighed as I took a sip of coffee from my travel mug with the words "I'm a Knotty Hooker" and a ball of yarn emblazoned on it.

I'd been watching my client's mother for over two hours now and gotten absolutely nada for my troubles. I hadn't been honest with my husband about where I was, but unlike the people I spent my time watching, I wasn't having an affair or even doing anything unsavory. Unless you consider being a dick unsavory.

A private dick, that is.

My name is Kitty Doolittle and I'm a stay-at-home mom by day and a private investigator by night. I didn't have a red Ferarri like Magnum but my minivan was like a sort of burgundy color especially when you took the rust stains into account, I haven't been able to wear shorts that short since college due to an unfortunate case of Mom-butt, and I did technically have a mustache that would make Selleck jealous but I waxed it off.

Menopause is a bitch.

We were living the Southern California, upper middle class high life: McMansion in a gated community, a luxury Mom-tank SUV, and His-and-Hers walk-in closets full of designer shoes.

Then my husband lost his job to corporate downsizing.

So we had to downsize our life. Now we live in a duplex and share a wall with a lady who has anywhere from thirteen to twenty seven chihuahuas. I drive a used minivan that, for some reason on a hot day, smells like a condom. And I share a closet with my husband. I was able to keep one pair of designer shoes: my black Christian Louboutin sneakers with silver studs.

Don't get me wrong. It wasn't the end of the world. We're not homeless, thank God. But things are different. It was important to us that I still be a stay-at-home mom, but that meant I had to find a way to supplement our income.

One afternoon I was having coffee with my best friend when she mentioned her daughter had been asked out by a boy. Within five minutes I found the Instagram his parents followed, the Snapchat that they didn't know about, his mother's old Myspace page and an article about his dad being arrested for streaking while drunk in the outfield at a baseball game twenty eight years ago.

She shook her head, chuckling. "Kitty, it's a shame you never became a cop, you would have been a great detective."

And I realized she was right. So I called in a favor to my old college roommate Barb, who was herself a cop now, took the test, got my concealed carry permit and faster than most of my clients finished in the bedroom with their secretaries I was an officially licensed Private Investigator.

The irony of my catching people in lies was that I myself was lying. My family didn't know about me working as a private investigator. Our family had already been through so much. First there had been the lifestyle change. Then there had been the cancer. I was diagnosed with breast cancer around the same time my husband lost his job. I'd had a single mastectomy, done some radiation, and now I was cancer-free. But we'd been through hell. This money was making a big difference for us and I was good at the work. There was no reason to make my husband worry more.

So I told my family I was selling Scentgasm candles (*"The scents that make you go 'Oooh!'"* *TM*) and now I got to do super-exciting, dangerous things like watch Henrietta Bolton's quaint little cottage house on its quaint little street in a quaint little part of town while pounding coffee in a desperate attempt to keep from nodding off.

It was exactly the kind of place you would expect an eighty-seven-year-old woman who wore "Oink-er Factory" sweaters and was really into crafting to live in. A pale pink house with lacy white trim, a barley sugar chimney, and French country shutters. I wanted to walk up to it and take a bite out of it, just to see if it was constructed from cookies and candy.

Although the lady who lived in that house turned out to be an evil witch who cannibalized children, so maybe not the best comparison because according to my client, his mother was the sweetest, most kind-hearted, generous woman to walk the face of the earth. So naturally, he was greatly concerned about the very young man his mother was dating.

"He's younger than me!" exclaimed Earl Bolton Jr. with disgust as we went over the case earlier that day in the hotel room. I didn't have an office because, oh yeah, that's right, my whole P.I. life was kind of a secret from my family.

"It's disgusting!" he continued. "I think she's giving him money. She's not rich, but my Dad was smart with their money. Some scuzzbag con artist type could see her as a target."

Unfortunately Earl didn't have much information on his mother's boyfriend. He didn't know his name and hadn't actually met him. He'd just seen the guy coming and going from the gingerbread house and when he'd asked his mother about it, she'd said she was seeing someone. Despite the fact that he was obviously a momma's boy, Earl's concern struck me as genuine and not self-serving. So I'd taken a description of the young stud, gotten my percentage upfront and started working on the case.

I'd been sitting here for two hours, and so far all I'd seen was a group of women around Henrietta's age come over for what appeared to be a crafting party. One of the good things about being me was that no one suspects the forty-something woman in the cat sweater sitting in the minivan of being up to no good.

A large van with an airbrushed mural of a cow doing ballet rolled up and parked with one tire up on the curb. The door opened and out stepped a rather scrubby-looking young white dude wearing baggy, ripped jeans and a sweatshirt that said "I" then a heart and a pink taco.

He matched the description Earl had given me of Henrietta's stud, so I snapped a few pictures using my fancy P.I. camera with the telescopic lens. Pink taco boy walked right in the front door like he owned the place, which I took as an opportunity to snap a few pictures of the van and get the plate number.

In a stroke of good luck, he'd left the doors unlocked, so I climbed in and snooped around. The first thing that hit me was the overwhelming scent of baking cookies and Bengay. Which, strangely, I didn't hate.

He'd left his wallet on the dashboard and inside I found one of those fake twenty-dollar bills with bible verses on it, a dill-pickle-flavored expired condom...WHAAAAT? And a driver's license that identified pink taco boy as Mr. Blarney Stone. Having been given a name like that, no wonder he had mommy issues.

Although, I suppose, being Kitty Doolittle I was one to talk.

In the glove box I found a ball of yarn, some knitting needles, registration that showed the van belonged to Henrietta and a loaded Glock. It even had a cute little knitted sweater-koozie on it. I had nothing against an old lady who lived alone having some protection but keeping it in the glove box was not exercising proper gun safety protocols.

Like the age of a tree is indicated by the number of rings, the layers of ever more grungy fast-food wrappers indicated that Blarney had been using the van for some time. The whole driver's area felt sticky and, in order to maintain my sanity, I chose not to dwell on the possible reasons for that.

I took a moment to relish sitting in the soft, gel-cushioned driver's seat, a stark contrast to my own that had a spring poking into my butt in a way that bordered on sexual assault.

Unfortunately, pink taco boy came out much sooner than I expected. I snorted as I joked to myself that he probably also came out much sooner than expected in the bedroom. Then I dove into the backseat of the van, pulled a blanket over myself and prayed he wasn't going to drive too far away from here.

He opened the passenger door, tossed something on the seat and got behind the wheel. It took everything I had not to gag out loud when I got a gust of air that smelled so rancid I was certain I was lying next to Henrietta's long-dead, rotting corpse. But it was just a bucket of ancient, moldy fried chicken.

Suddenly Blarney shouted a curse word, hopped out of the car and ran back inside.

I praised my luck but couldn't leave just yet. A large, pink duffel bag sat on the passenger seat. I opened the bag to get a look inside and could hardly believe what lay before me. I grabbed one and put it in my pocket then slid back out of the car. As I was closing the driver's door, he came out.

"Hey! What'er ya doin' to my car?" he demanded as he marched over to me.

Fortunately I'd brought my cellphone to snap the car pictures, so I was able to improvise.

"Just taking a selfie with your sweet ride!" I said with way too much enthusiasm, then made duck face as I took a picture.

He stared at me with a dumbfounded look. "Uh, what's up with your tittie?"

Looking down, I saw that my left breast insert was down by my stomach. Sometimes this dang thing had a mind of its own. I adjusted it back into the proper place. "Oh, you know, you get older and they sag like a wet sack of potatoes."

He made a disgusted face and opened the driver's door. "Whatever, lady. Beat it."

"Cool sweatshirt," I said. "I love tacos, too!"

"I'll bet you do," he sneered, then slammed the door.

As I watched him peel away, I felt more confused. I'd expected the duffel to be filled with money or valuables. Instead it was filled with…

Glitter glue.

3.

My six-year-old, Hannah, was gluing cotton balls to a poster at the kitchen counter. My ten-year-old, Mark, was building a diorama at the dining room table. And my fourteen-year-old, Charlotte, sat on the couch in the living room adjacent to the kitchen doing her homework. My brain was a bit overwhelmed running back and forth between Hannah, Mark, and the stove, so when Charlotte asked me a question, I didn't really listen and just said yes.

"Oh my God! Mom! Why do you have porn open on your computer?" exclaimed Charlotte loudly.

"What?" I asked, confused, dropping the spoon I was using into the boiling spaghetti pot.

"Shart!" I spat.

"What's a 'shart', Mommy?" asked Hannah.

"Nothing," I said. "It's a bad word. Sort of. Charlotte, why are you on my computer?" I demanded, closing the short distance to where she sat at the counter. I slapped my laptop lid down and snatched up the computer.

Then I cursed myself silently for leaving up the pictures I'd taken of a client's husband *in flagrante delicto* with his secretary. I wasn't sure what bothered me more: that he was the scumbag she suspected him to be or that he was such an unimaginative scumbag. Having sex with your much younger secretary was so 1955. This is the 21st century; have an affair with the bi-curious barista at your local hookah bar slash coffee shop or something.

"It's not porn Charlotte, it's art…mock-up art for a new Scentgasm candles ad campaign."

"Gross," she said.

"What's 'porn', Mommy?" asked Hannah.

"It's another bad word, sweetie," I said. "Sort of. So let's not repeat it...wait, what are you using to glue your cotton balls?" I asked her as I noticed what she held in her hand.

"This cool glitter glue I found in your purse!" she exclaimed happily. "I ran out of white glue."

"Okay honey," I said as I gently took it from her. "Please don't just grab things out of my purse, okay?" I handed her some glue I found in the utility drawer and went back to the nearly boiling-over spaghetti. Hannah had overdone it with the glue and it was dribbling down the side of the container. A dollop of it plopped off onto the stove where the flame from the burner caught it. Then there was an explosion.

* * * * *

The only thing that didn't survive the explosion was my eyebrows. Well...and my dignity. The next morning I had to draw them on.

"You know," said my husband, "if we got you a checkered flannel and some ten-inch hoop earrings you could really complete this look."

"I will cut you," I said.

"See, you're even in character! That's hot," he teased.

After dropping the kids off at school, I went to the police station to meet up with my cop friend Barb. She was not what a perp expected when Detective Barbara "Barbwire" Hardmont walked into the interrogation room.

Barb was a former kindergarten teacher who switched career paths into police work because she wanted a little more excitement in her job. She was soft and cuddly looking and gave off this aura that made you want to ask her to give you a hug. But in the interrogation room she would trip you up, until your story was so tangled and mangled that you hung yourself.

Hence the nickname Barbwire.

"I guess P.I. work isn't paying enough, eh?" Barb asked when I walked into her office.

"It pays fine," I said, confused.

"Then what's up with the mime look?"

"My husband is into mimes."

"TMI, girl." She laughed then looked over the file I'd handed her. "So this Blarney Stone fella has a rap sheet for possession, shoplifting, and...selling taxidermied exotic animals over state lines," Barb said as she looked over the background check I'd run on him. "He seems to have a *rocky* relationship with the law," she quipped.

"Yeah he's a real *gem*," I joked back. "Anyway, as I explained on the phone, since glitter glue generally does not explode when exposed to flames, I'm hoping your crime lab peeps can figure out exactly what it is."

I guessed it was some kind of drug, and that Blarney was somehow using Henrietta as a cover for his criminal activities. To use a sweet old lady in a dangerous crime like drug dealing was a whole new level of low. I wanted to get this sleazebag. Barb said it could take awhile to run the substance, but she'd get back to me.

Then I went back and parked outside Henrietta Bolton's house. I had to roll up my windows because there was a public pool across the street and there were a bunch of kids in it playing "Marco-Polo" at full volume, making it hard to concentrate.

When Blarney Stone showed up again, I decided to see if I could figure out what he was up to inside that house. I waited until he was in, then I got out of my van, crept up carefully to the house and made my way around to the side yard. At the first window I peeked into, I saw two old ladies doing crafts in the living room. Nothing out of the ordinary.

When I got to the back window, I saw that most of the other women in Henrietta's craft club were in the kitchen, and they weren't baking cookies. It appeared they were cooking...

Drugs.

I pulled my phone out to snap a few pictures, then I was going to get the heck out of here. This was above my pay grade. But just as I snapped the last photo I felt a sharp pain on the back of my head and everything went black.

4.

When I came to, I found myself tied to a rocking chair in what appeared to be the basement. It was fully finished and decorated in pastel colors with lots of crocheted doilies and blankets tossed over the dated furniture. It would have been nice, except for the maze created by floor-to-ceiling stacks of newspapers. My wrists and legs were secured to the chair with pink yarn. There was something shoved in my mouth and a scarf was tied around my head to keep it in there.

Standing before me were Henrietta Bolton, Blarney Stone, and another old woman in a mu-mu who was knitting. Well, technically Henrietta was sitting on her walker, but you get the idea. There was a metal TV tray set up in front of me. On it were a large wooden spoon, a bottle of hot sauce and a jug of castor oil.

"Untie her gag," said Henrietta. Blarney came over and removed my gag, then I spit out what they'd shoved in my mouth.

"Is that soap?" I asked angrily.

"Naughty girls get their mouths washed out with soap," said Henrietta. "This is her, Blarney?"

"Yeah, this is the broad who was snooping around the van yesterday."

She grabbed the wooden spoon and swatted Blarney's hand. "You will not refer to ladies as 'broads' in my home, young man!"

"Shit!" he complained. "That hurt, Mrs. Bolton!"

She sighed. "Get the sauce, Blarney."

He hung his head. "Yes ma'am," then he grabbed the hot sauce off the TV tray and Henrietta put a large dollop on his tongue.

"You hold that there, don't you swallow it young man, and you think about more appropriate words you can use to express yourself. Now," she said. "This is the woman you think took it?" she asked him. He nodded, his tongue hanging out of his mouth like when a cartoon character sees a hot chick.

"Where is it, young lady?" she asked me.

"Where is what?"

"Don't think you can pull one over on me. I may be old but I'm sharp as a tack."

"I don't know what you're talking about," I said.

She walked over to the table and carefully poured the castor oil onto a large silver spoon.

"Muriel, grab her head," she said to the woman who was knitting.

Muriel set aside her work and shuffled over to me. She wrapped her surprisingly strong hands around my head and held me still. Then Henrietta came over with the spoon and made me swallow the castor oil.

It tasted like sautéed feet.

"You're old enough to know that castor oil will give you the runs. And I'll bet my next Social Security check you're menopausal and if you're having the diarrhea like I had then you certain as cinnamon don't want to swallow any more. So 'fess up and let's be done with this silliness."

"You know," shouted Muriel at the top of her lungs.

"For heaven's sake, Muriel, fix your hearing aid!"

Muriel reached up and adjusted, causing a high-pitched sound to nearly deafen me.

"You know, I thought I was menopausal because I was having the diarrhea too, but it turned out I had ovarian cancer."

"They thay the road to ovarian canther is paved with Pepto-Bismol," Blarney said with a lisp because his tongue was still hanging out of his mouth. We all stared at him with surprise. "My grandma had it," he said.

"I'm sorry to hear that," I said sincerely. "Cancer sucks."

"Yeth, it duth," he said, a large splurb of drool gushing out.

"All right, all right, now tell me where it is!" snapped Henrietta.

I didn't know what she was talking about. When I didn't answer she gave me another spoonful of castor oil. I started coughing and it came spurting out my nose, which burned something awful.

"Darlin', what in tarnation did you do to your eyebrows?" asked Muriel. "You don't think that looks good, do you?"

My eyebrows...the explosion...the glitter glue!

"The glitter glue...isn't glitter glue, is it?" I asked.

"You're smarter than you look," said Henrietta.

"But why? Why would you all be making drugs?" I knew it wasn't drugs, but I was hoping to get her to tell me what it was.

"Drugs?" she asked then looked at Blarney and Muriel and shared a laugh. "Maybe you're actually dumber than you look."

I waited.

"Sweet cheeks, we're making explosives and selling them to terrorists."

Well you could knock me over with a feather. I sure wasn't expecting that answer. "But...*why*?" I croaked.

"Medicare supplemental insurance only goes so far," said Henrietta.

"My heart pills are one thousand dollars a month!" snapped Muriel. "I live on a fixed income! How am I supposed to afford that?"

"So that justifies helping people commit murder?" I asked angrily. In my anger I tensed up and an incredibly long, loud fart escaped me. Everyone went silent.

"That wath juthy," Blarney lisped disgustedly.

"The castor oil is working quickly. I'm going to let you sit down here and suffer a bit. Maybe in twenty minutes you'll be ready to talk in order to get some relief."

"Or you'll have a helluva mess to clean up," said Blarney.

Henrietta slapped his wrists again then grabbed the soap. "That's it young man, you put this in your mouth and go to the corner," she said as they all went upstairs.

I wasn't going to sit down here for twenty minutes, waiting to be force-fed more laxative. I was able to turn my body just enough to look behind me and saw a pair of scissors on a craft table. So I started rocking the chair, forcing it to scoot along gold shag carpet. Unfortunately I rocked too forcefully and tipped myself back and over. A stack of newspapers came tumbling down onto me.

"Shart!" I exclaimed as I struggled against the yarn. It frayed as I twisted my wrists beneath it, in an attempt to loosen it. All I got for my trouble was hot, burning pain as the yarn cut into my skin. I kicked my legs to try to upright the chair and my eye caught on my shoes. My trusty black, studded Louboutin hightop sneakers.

I managed to use one foot to slip the shoe off my other foot. It fell and hit me in the face, cutting my cheek and confirming the sharpness of those studs. I got the shoe into my hand and used the stud to fray the yarn until it snapped. Then I freed my other hand, clamored up out of the rocker and ran up the stairs.

Where I found myself face to face with a gun.

* * * * *

"Henrietta! That's your glue gun!" shouted Muriel, as she came up behind me and pressed the knitting needle to my jugular vein.

"Dagnabit. I need to check my prescription," Henrietta called to the other room. "Esther, you grabbed my Glock instead of the glue gun!"

A single gunshot sounded from the living room. Then a little old lady in a cat sweater shuffled into the room, traded the Glock for the glue gun and shuffled back out muttering about her ruined cat figurine.

"Last chance, sugar," Henrietta said menacingly.

I shook my head. "I don't have it."

"Stop lying to us, young lady," said Muriel, pressing a knitting needle harder against my neck.

"My God, woman, you have strong hands," I croaked.

"I was Miss Happy Injun Butter 1947, '48, and '49. I destroyed the other girls in the butter churn event. Churnin' kept the arthritis away."

"That's an incredibly racist brand name," I said.

"Enough!" shouted Hernrietta. "There was ten thousand dollars worth of product in that bottle you took. So unless you can cough up ten grand, prepare to shake hands with Jesus."

Then she raised the gun to fire.

Like I said earlier, the casserole I had cooking in the crock pot for dinner popped into my head. It seems stupid, but what that made me think of next was not being around to eat that dinner together with my family. Then the thought of my kids waiting outside their schools for a mom who would never pick them up. Then the thought of my husband having to do life alone.

The breast cancer didn't kill me. This old bat wasn't about to either.

There were a bunch of crafting supplies on the nearby dining table. The scissors were out of my reach, but there was one other option.

I wrapped my hands around a bottle of glitter and threw it in the faces of Muriel, Blarney and

Henrietta. They shrieked in pain as they tried to blink the glitter out of their eyes.

"It feels like broken glass!" shrieked Blarney in a girlishly high voice.

"Glitter is the herpes of crafting, bitches!" I yelled, then made a run for it.

Henrietta managed to trip me. I scrambled back up but before I could run, she plunged that knitting needle into my chest.

Fortunately it was into my left side and straight into my fake boob insert. We both stood for a long beat staring at the knitting needle sticking out of my chest, looking like something out of a horror movie that was so low-budget it couldn't afford any blood effects. Before either of us could make another move, the sound of helicopter blades cutting the air filled the room.

"Henrietta Bolton," said a familiar voice through a loudspeaker. "We have you surrounded. Come out with your hands up!"

"It's over, Henrietta," I said.

"That's what you think," she said, then she grabbed Blarney by the arm and they both ran down into the basement, just as Barb kicked in the door and rushed in. I put my hands up. Barb had her gun pointed at me, but relaxed when she realized it was me.

"Kitty?" she asked with surprise. Then she looked at my boob. "Why the hell do you have a knitting needle stuck in your boob?"

5.

I was sitting on the back of the ambulance with a blanket around my shoulders when Barb approached me.

"They got away," said Barb dejectedly.

"What!" I exclaimed. "How?"

"The maze of newspapers slowed us down and gave them time to go out a window in the back. We found it open."

"I can't picture Henrietta Bolton getting out of a window," I said. "Not with her needing a walker to get around…"

"Excuse me. Lieutenant Wilson?" said a young officer to Barb. "We swept the backyard and the surrounding block. There's no sign of them."

"Okay, thanks Officer Marco," she said. Then she turned to me. "Well, I guess we're out of luck for the night."

"Dammit," I said, as I looked around. My eye caught on the public pool across the street. "Wait a minute," I said. "I have an idea."

* * * * *

Barb went down ahead of me, gun drawn, and did a quick sweep of the area.

"So what's this big idea?" she asked.

I put my finger to my lips and walked to the center of the basement.

"Marco!" I yelled loudly.

"Polo!" said Blarney loudly.

"Shut up, you idiot!" snapped Henrietta. But it was too late. Barb was on them. She yanked down a bunch of newspapers and moved a dresser out of the way to reveal a crawlspace where Blarney and Henrietta were crouched uncomfortably.

Henrietta glared at me with her cold, angry eyes.

"Winner, winner, chicken dinner," I said.

6.

As I pulled up to the front of the high school after waiting in the pickup line that wound around the block, I didn't see Charlotte in the usual spot she waited for me. I looked around the large courtyard in front of the school and spotted her near the flagpole talking to a tall, handsome boy.

"Mommy, why does Charlotte keep throwing her head around like that? Is there a bug in her face?" asked Hannah in the backseat.

"No sweetie, she's fine." I beeped the horn once and Charlotte made an awkward goodbye gesture to the guy and came over.

"You're gonna get whiplash if you keep tossing your hair around him like that," I teased.

"I don't know what you're talking about," she said primly.

"Why are you so sweaty?" asked Mark.

"I am not!" she snapped.

"Look at your pits, dude. You look like you armpit farted a couple of water balloons," he said.

"Shut up, turd!" she said.

"All right, that's enough," I said as Mark and Hannah started laughing and armpit farting.

When we got home, the little kids ran inside but Charlotte stopped me. "Mom...can I ask you something?"

"Sure, what's up?"

"How do you know if a guy likes you?" she asked, shyly.

The sudden urge to hug her and never let go took hold of me. I looked at her and saw my little girl, and while she wasn't really little anymore, she still needed me.

And I'd almost died today.

I swallowed the lump in my throat but couldn't stop the tears from filling up my eyes.

"Oh my God! Don't be all weird about it! Never mind!" she said and started to get out.

"No!" I said, grabbing her arm. "It's just hormones. Stupid menopause. Why don't we go inside, I'll send the other kids up to their rooms to do their homework and we can talk about it."

She rolled her eyes but smiled. "Okay."

"Sooooo...what's his name?"

"Jacob."

"His full name, including middle."

"God Mom, you're so weird."

It would have made the background check so much easier, but that was okay. I would figure it out because I am...

Kitty Doolittle: Stay-at-Home P.I.

Jennifer Milne's short fiction has appeared in CinderQ magazine, Mysterion Online, The Arcanist and others. Her screenplay THE CONSCRIPTION won multiple awards in festivals in 2019 and her Y.A. romance *CUPID'S KISS* is published by Rogue Phoenix Press. She lives in San Diego with her family.

The Tale of an Indentured Marine

Jedwin Smith

Marine Corps Recruit Depot-San Diego. We're talking ancient history. Pat Boone was still relevant, as were LBJ, cigarettes, and drive-in theaters.

It was June 1964 and five dozen or so of us teenage misfits were suffering through our initial days of boot camp, which was as close to a thirteen-week stint in Hell as any of us had yet ever experienced. Vietnam was still two years distant.

Our DI (drill instructor) — half-Puerto Rican, half-Neanderthal — rarely spoke. He mostly screamed, constantly reminding us we were "raggedy-assed" handfuls of human excrement. Depending on the day of the week, we were a friggin' mob, maggots, or motherless scum. Individually, we were called "Boots".

Our days began in darkness at 0530 and concluded in collapsed "lights out" exhaustion at 2200 hours. And during that nine hundred ninety minutes in between we ran and did everything else by the numbers — pushups, squat thrusts, chin-ups — and then we ran some more. To break the monotony, we learned the intricacies of our M-14 rifles, the legendary history of the Corps, and mastered close-order drill on a blacktopped quadrant called The Grinder.

We ate together, hit the head together, ran together, and marched together. Everything in unison. Teamwork the order of the day. No room for individualism. The Corps eliminated our independence and rebuilt us to its Gung Ho specs; no longer did we take time to think about the pros and cons of any and all situations — instead, we did as ordered. Without question.

Ours was a joyless environment. But at the end of the tunnel — after ninety one days of near-insanity that chiseled us into lean, mean fighting machines — were those awesome dress blues. Lady magnets if there ever was one.

Boot camp instilled in us a new language. I'm not referring to swearing, although a Marine's coarse vocabulary is legendary. A wall was not a wall; it was a bulkhead. Ditto a toilet, which was a head. The floor was the deck, which we hit with monotonous regularity — daily pushups by the hundreds. We didn't wear hats; we wore covers. Pants were what women wore; we wore trousers. We didn't dine in a cafeteria; we chowed down in a mess hall. We didn't sleep in a bed; we grunts referred to it as a rack.

For entertainment, we fought each other — under strict supervision, however. With padded clubs, hand-to-hand tactics, simulated bayonet drills. We smaller boots were always paired against the bigger dudes in order to pummel the fear factor out of us. Those who wavered, who never could quite get with the program, were a detriment to us all. If one boot screwed up, the entire platoon paid the price, usually with seemingly endless push-ups. Or, worse yet, our "smoking lamp" would be canceled. Indeed, we came to believe that somewhere in that "Guidebook for Marines" that we lived by, it said cigarette depredation helped build teamwork.

A boot would drop his rifle, God help him. Or briefly stand under the shower spigot and refuse to apply soap. Or maybe his footlocker wasn't in proper order. The infractions were mind-numbing, the punishment soul-sapping. You either learned quickly or…well, the DI would call us to attention and, in a thundering voice, ask, "So, maggots, what the hell are we gonna do about that shitbird?"

In one instance, I took matters into my own hands. Truth be known, it haunts me to this day…

I remember him as Lush-shiana, the hyphen meaning he slurred much of his speech. He was a massive, big-boned kid. A swamp critter born down on the bayou. A Purple Tiger fan of Louisiana State University, always rattling on about Billy Cannon. Anyway, the dude's slurring was due to a mouthful of bad teeth. No, I take that back; he had a mouthful of rotten teeth. Which I had no way of knowing at the time until that fateful early-morning moment during our eighth or ninth day in Hell. Out there on The Grinder, asshole to belly button, running in lockstep — left, right, left, by the numbers. All of us scared shitless, fearing the wrath of our DI for some real or imagined screw-up.

Besides being born with two left feet, Lush-shiana also had the IQ of a squirrel. You have to understand that, until the advent of today's computerized battlefield, the Corps wasn't looking to recruit Rhodes Scholars. They wanted knuckleheads they could convince to willingly charge enemy machine gun emplacements. Dudes who idolized John Wayne, he of Sgt. Stryker fame in the movie "Sands of Iwo Jima". Hooligans who would kill for the honor of being a Marine.

Most of us fit the bill. The majority could read and write, had had our difficulties at home and with the police. Above all else, most of us joined for the opportunity to legally break things and hurt people. And get paid to do it. What a deal, huh?

Lush-shiana, however, was…well, in today's parlance, he was problematic. Back in the day I swore he was mentally deficient — constantly confused, especially when it came to differentiating his left foot from his right. Which is hell on wheels when it comes to running in lockstep formation. Especially when Lush-shiana was plodding along, directly behind me. And forever stepping on my heels.

Clomp! And I almost fell on my face into the boot in front of me, who screamed, "Bust that bastard."

Clomp! Tripped again, this time yelling to Lush-shiana to get in step.

But he didn't, instead nailing my heel again, sending me stumbling forward. Which prompted the dude in front of me to fire an elbow into my chest. Quick-tempered like I was in those days, I spun around and fired a straight right fist into Lush-shiana's mouth.

This, followed by a scream from the galoot and what seemed like a geyser of blood and teeth.

Gee-zus! Then all hell broke loose. Lush-shiana dropped to his knees, taking a couple of stumbling boots with him. Chaos as the platoon broke ranks, and our DI going ballistic: "What the fuck's goin' on here? Whoa, herd, whoa. Smith, what the hell happened, you turd?"

Long story short, ol' Lush-shiana was hustled off to sick call, where Navy corpsmen did their best to clean up his wound, and then days later the DI informed us that the Navy dental folks were addressing the lad's problem. With no further explanation forthcoming, the smoking lamp was lit. And from that moment on, the rest of the boots gave me a wide berth. Hell, I felt like John Wayne himself. I was bulletproof. Invincible. Best yet, the DI appointed me squad leader.

Problem was, Lush-shiana would soon be rejoining the platoon, which I dreaded. This big-boned, swamp-raised critter probably wrestled gators back home in his spare time. In a fair fight, he'd kick the shit out of me. So all I could do was fret about his return, get my affairs in order, and await Armageddon.

And then, several days later, here he came. His shadow darkening the Platoon Street. Godzilla blocking out the sun. A-runnin' toward us, his big-booted feet actually working in synch, his immensely muscled arms a-flyin', and his steely eyes afire.

Admittedly, confusion set in at this point. In my mind's eye, I saw my mother back home lighting a candle in church for the redemption of my soul. All the while I'm praying for forgiveness of my sins: Hail Mary, full of grace, pray for us sinners...as I rigidly awaited a greatly-deserved ass-kicking.

But no way was I going down without a fight. With fists clenched, I stared down the enemy, just like John Wayne did on those fabled Iwo Jima sands. By God, I too was going to die with my boots on.

And just like that, in the blink of an eye — no, in the magnanimous flash of a wide-mouthed toothy grin — ol' Lush-shiana wrapped me in a bone-crushing hug and shouted over and over: "Thank you, thank you, I'm a-thankin' you…"

That Louisiana swamp dweller had been plagued by bad teeth all his short-lived life. "Bad tooths and gum ailments, no end in sight," he said. "And then youse hep'd me out, me gettin' to dem dentist folk 'hed o' schedule. Deys jerked out the rest o' 'ems bad'ens an' gives me a new mouthfuls of tooths."

To prove the point, he grabbed me by the shoulders and jaw-jutted a pristine mouthful of dentures before my startled eyes. "Jes looky here, sees for yuz'selfs. So's I's a-thankin' you. Can't thanks you 'nuff," he said, releasing his fearsome grip.

With a straight face, I said, "Ah…my pleasure, Boot."

Never did call him Lush-shiana again. Which is how I lived to fight another day.

Jedwin Smith has battled malaria and evaded Soviet and Ethiopian soldiers to become a 1986 Pulitzer Prize finalist for his coverage of the war in East Africa.

He's compared battle scars with great motorcycle daredevil Evel Knievel and had a near-death experience bringing Spanish gold, silver, and emeralds to the surface from the fabled treasure galleon Atocha.

He is the author of *Our Brother's Keeper*, *Let's Get It On! The Mills Lane Story*, and *Fatal Treasure*.

I AM ISRAEL — Lions and Lambs of the Land was released in 2018 from Blue Room Books.

JedwinSmith.com

Toes

Roy Richardson

I have two hands and two feet, with five fingers and five toes each. They all match. This is a very symmetrically pleasing arrangement. My Momma says this is proof of God's Divine Plan. In my head I answer that it is proof of the efficiency of bilateral symmetry in a random evolutionary environment. I nearly always have good in-my-head answers.

I learned to give answers in my head after I gave Momma one of my out-loud smart-ass answers and she smacked me even after Dr. Terri had told her not to. She mostly only does that when she's drunk. I try not to talk to her when she's been drinking, but that is when she always wants to talk the most.

It is also the only time she calls me a GD retard.

My Momma says my face is disconnected from my brain because I don't cry when she spanks me. The fact that she sometimes says things that make sense is very confusing to me. "Inconsistent" is the word my last therapist, Dr. Terri, taught me. I liked Dr. T; she was very consistent, but she was not symmetrical. She had short, stumpy fingers but long, skinny toes. This was so distracting that I had trouble listening to her. Maybe that is why Dr. Terri sent me to a more symmetrical therapist.

I like my new therapist, Dr. Anderson. She is very symmetrical. Her hands and feet match, her nails are never broken, and the polish she puts on them is not too bright — and is never chippy. *Subtle* is the word she taught me for this.

Even though Dr. Anderson is nice to me and smiles a lot, she has Sad Eyes. I hope she is not sad because she knows better than anyone what a GD retard I am.

Momma does not like Dr. Anderson. She says that she is a prissy little b-word that has never worked hard a day in her life. Momma says the same thing about all my therapists, except for Dr. Harris, who she called a prissy little p-word because he was a man.

My Momma works at Waffle House. She calls it that GD H-hole, but I like it when she goes to work there, because she has to wear tennis shoes that cover up her bright red, chippy toenail polish. She smells good when she comes home, like waffles and bacon. She even brings me stuff to eat sometimes. Maybe it is a GD H-hole, but they make good waffles. I like apple cinnamon best.

Once, I was unsubtle enough to complain about my Momma's chippy toenail polish when she was drunk. She told me if I ever said anything like that again, she was going to cut my f'ing toes off with the big butcher knife she keeps hidden under the sink so that no one can break in and kill us with it.

We saw this happen on one of the "Pain and Death" shows she likes to watch. That's not what they're really called, but that is what my older brother Aaron calls them. He says this because he can't remember what the real names are. He says if I were not an f'ing retard, I would understand. He says I have no sense of humor. I answer in my head that I do too have a sense of humor, I can always sense when people are laughing at me. I think I'd be better off without a sense of humor.

I might be a retard, but I am not stupid, no matter what Aaron says. I have an IQ of 135. It's just that so much of what normal people say and do makes no GD sense to me.

For example, even though I know what "smart-ass" means, the term is ridiculous (BTW, I will say "ass" because it is in the Bible, and so it is not profanity, though I do get confused as to when it is appropriate or not). The buttocks, while containing the largest muscles in the human body and working very efficiently for walking and sitting, have not a thing to do with the human cognitive process. It would be much more logical to call them stupid-ass answers, even though they are really not.

I try to have good manners, because I think God punishes you if you don't. Once, I went into Aaron's room without knocking, and on his computer I saw naked people sucking on each other's toes. It was the most awful thing I could imagine, worse than any "Pain and Death" show ever, but I couldn't stop watching. Aaron screamed at me when he came out of the bathroom, and slammed his laptop shut. He made me promise not to say a word to Momma, and to always knock before coming into a room.

If he knew me at all, he would have understood that there was no way I could discuss something like that with Momma, or anyone else, not even Dr. Anderson. Especially not Dr. Anderson.

As it was, I dreamed for weeks of choking on giant, dirty toes.

I have a good memory. I can remember almost everything that has ever happened to me. For example, I remember when I was five and a yellow jacket stung me. It hurt a lot but I didn't cry, because I was trying to be a big boy like my brother Aaron. But then he told me that yellow jackets were poison like black widow spiders, and that I was going to die. I still didn't cry, but then he explained to me how after I died, they'd put me in the ground and worms would eat my eyeballs, and everyone would forget me, and I wouldn't even go to heaven because Jesus don't love fat little retards.

I think it was the part about the worms eating my eyeballs that finally got to me, because I didn't believe the part about Jesus, but I just couldn't stand the idea of going to heaven with no eyeballs. So I cried and cried, even after Momma shook me and screamed at me to please in the name of God to shut the f up. When I finally told them why I couldn't stop, Deddy took off his belt and whipped me and Aaron good.

I stopped crying then because listening to Aaron boo-hoo took my mind off my eyeballs.

Deddy left a few years after that. Momma got real drunk and told me it was 'cause I was a GD retard, but I told her I knew it was 'cause Deddy's sperm was too old. This was before I had learned to answer in my head. I thought she might spank me, but she got a funny look on her face and asked me why I thought that.

I told her that I'd heard her and Deddy discussing it one night after I was in bed but couldn't sleep because they were not using their Inside Voices in this discussion. Deddy had said I was the way I was because Momma had drunk alcohol while she was pregnant with me. Momma said Uh-uh, that wasn't it, 'cause she hadn't drunk that much, and besides, she'd just seen something on Fox News that proved that Asperger's was caused by older men having weak sperm. And Deddy had said GD, you always bring that age thing up, but have you looked in the mirror lately, you ain't exactly a spring chicken yourself. Then Momma said Mebbe not, but I'll always be younger than you.

Then the door slammed, and it got real quiet, except for Momma crying, and then I went to sleep.

When I finished telling this, Momma went and got another beer and took a long drink, but this did not make the funny look go away. Then she said Now hunny, it's like this, and I knew then I was in for a lot of talk either about old things that I had heard before or new things that would make no sense to me.

She started in on God's Will and Jesus' Love and being good to get to heaven, and all the things I'd heard a million times before, and I started staring at her chippy toes, and before I even knew it I'd said I couldn't understand what all that had to do with Deddy's sperm being too old.

Momma slapped me, then reached out and grabbed my face in one of her man-hands and hollered Stop lookin' at my GD toes! You look me right in the eyes, Little Man, and you listen to what I'm telling you! She was squeezing my face real hard, and for once I couldn't think of a smart or even stupid-assed answer, so I just looked her in the eyes and said OK.

Then she turned me loose and said, Little Man, you have got to learn to put a zipper on that smart-ass mouth of yours if you don't want to go through life gettin' yore ass whupped on a reg'lar basis. I started to argue, but she grabbed my face again with one man-hand, and made a zipping motion across her mouth with the other, saying Got it?

I nodded and she let me go.

She took another long drink, looked at me with her Hard Eyes, and then told me something that changed my life. Think about it like this, she said. You understand about using your Inside Voice, right? I nodded, concentrating hard on not looking at her toes. Well then, she said, use your Inside Voice in your head, understand? Instead of just blabbing out the first smart-ass thing that comes to mind, use your Inside Voice to say it to yourself in your own head, awright?

I have to confess that I was awestruck by this revelatory concept. The fact that it had come from Momma was even more astounding. Maybe there was something to her oft-repeated "I might be ignernt, but I ain't stupid" phrase after all, chippy toenails or not.

And I have to admit, my life got a lot easier after I learned to answer in my head. Like when Momma would start going on about a just God condemning Deddy to burn in H forever, I'd say — in my head — that if there were a just God, I wouldn't have to live in a double-wide in Alabama with a drunk-assed Momma who slaps me with her man-hands and torments me with her bright red chippy toenail polish. And the very fact that Momma herself had come up with a way that I could make smart-ass answers and not get an ass-whuppin' made me smile in my head.

Sometimes I do think that maybe there is a just God after all.

My Momma says there are some mean-assed motherf'ers in this world. And while the Pain and Death shows provide plenty of evidence for this statement, we have yet to see one showing a motherf'er mean enough to cut off a little boy's toes with a butcher knife.

Writer/artist Roy Richardson hasn't had a real job in over thirty years, except for four years of teaching, which proved to be a mistake.

He and his wife currently illustrate the long-running syndicated comic strip "Mary Worth", which leaves him one day a week for writing — if he keeps up with his deadlines.

facebook.com/hillbilliespreferblondes/

A MawMaw, a Bear Claw, and a Messy Chaw

P.V. Rose

Folks at work call me Brawley but MawMaw called me Robert Brawley Cateswin. Every mornin' she used to holler down the hall at six oh clock. She say Robert Brawley Cateswin you smell that coffee and I holler back Yes I do MawMaw and she say I ain't no cow so you call me Mother and I say Yes MawMaw. MawMaw once said that was our little joke but she don't call me no more because she died and now I get my coffee ev'r' mornin' at the Waffle House.

The Waffle House has coffee that is almost as good as MawMaw's. They knows Imma comin' and every mornin' when I get there they say Hey Brawley and I say hey and they say Here's your coffee and Your usual? And I say thank you and yes and by the time I get to the high seat in front of the man who does the cookin' my coffee is sittin' there just a-waitin' on me and it is good coffee.

I have the same thing to eat every day because I like it. One day this lady says to me she says Hey Brawley why don't you try the waffle and I said I like the patty melt — they make it on raisin toast for me — and the hash browns and cheesy eggs too and she said Hey Brawley I was just kiddin' but it weren't funny.

So after breakfast at the Waffle House I go to work but I walk to work because I do not have a car and even if I did I do not know how to drive which is why MawMaw's car is still sittin' under the portico next to the house. Some fella at work said he would buy it but he asked for the paperwork for the car and I did not know of what he talked so he didn't buy it.

I been workin' since I quit school. There was no cause for me to go to school. MawMaw used to tell me she'd say Robert Brawley Cateswin you are slow but you have a good heart and don't let anybody ever tell you otherwise. She was all for me quittin' school and gettin' a job because she said she thought workin' at the cotton plant in Alto would make me happy. MawMaw was right.

I love workin' at the cotton plant.

I started at the cotton plant when I was sixteen and I am now fifty years old…at least I think I am. Every year on my birthday MawMaw would make me a cake and take it to the cotton plant and surprise me and everybody would get a slice of the cake. MawMaw sure knew how to make a cake. And the cake would say Happy Birthday Robert Brawley Cateswin you are…and then I would know how old I was. So the last cake she made said

I was forty seven and somebody at work said she sure did miss my MawMaw's cake and ain't I fifty years old now and I agreed but I'm just not sure.

My job at the cotton plant is made just for me. My boss said so. He said Brawley you ain't got much upstairs but you're a strong fella and what do you think about pushin' these heavy carts for the little ladies who ain't got much muscle and I thought it was a fine thing and that's what I been doin' since I was sixteen. I push carts with cotton bales on them and I push carts with big spools full of rope cotton on them and I push carts with little spindles of thread on them.

Everybody knows me in every department because somebody always got a heavy cart that needs movin'. Brawley! they holler and I come a-runnin'. I don't run like I used to because MawMaw told me that I was gettin' older and would slow down and that was natural and not to worry about it. But they still like me at work even if I am slow every which way. I push full carts from cardin' over to spinnin' and from spinnin' over to weavin' and empty carts too. My shoes is loaded with travelers and I pick them out every day after I get home from work.

I've had a lot of bosses. Right now I've got a fellow by the name of Dug. That is a funny name. Dug. Dug. Dug. I don't know why his ma would name him after a hole in the ground but mamas are sometimes funny like that. Dug seems to walk around a lot. He mostly talks to the womens. They must have very fun jobs because he's always at their workstations just a-talkin' and a-laughin' with them and well I might be slow but I think them ladies likes Dug as a boss. Dug always slaps me on the back and says How's it goin' Brawley? It's always goin' good and I say so and Dug nods his head and say he's happy 'bout dat and I like to make Dug happy so I keep sayin' it.

But there is one thing I'm not happy about. Used to be a long time ago my other boss Charlie had somethin' he called Brawley's Bear Claw Friday. Charlie's wife had a bakery and Charlie would bring in food from her bakery. He'd come to me and he'd say Brawley I need your muscles reckon you can help me haul in some boxes and I knew what he was talkin' about and I'd say Sure and I would help him take boxes of donuts around to all the breakrooms.

Charlie's wife always made a bag just for me. Charlie told her how I sure did like them world-famous bear claws of hers and next thing I knew every Friday was Brawley's Bear Claw Friday. But then Charlie retired and I never did know where that lady's shop was and I didn't get no more bear claws since then. Dug does not bring me any bear claws but other than that he's pretty nice so I tell him everythin's going good.

I sure do miss my bear claws. If the Waffle House had bear claws I surely would buy me one every day.

One day this pretty little girl comes to work and she's workin' in the spinnin' department. I knew she was extra special because all the big bosses from the front office used to come out and talk to her. Mostly the big bosses just walked around and looked and waved but didn't talk to nobody except Dug. Dug is a short fellow and when he talks to me he always has to look way up because I am tall. Dug has to look up at the big bosses too but I don't have to because I'm tall like the big bosses.

So this pretty little girl was needin' some help one day with a heavy thing and somebody told her to go find Brawley and tell me what to do. This little girl she hot-footed it everywhere she went. She was fast and quick and the big bosses had a heck of a time cornerin' her for a chat. So here she come a-hot-footin' over my way and she looked up at me and she said Are you Brawley? I opened my mouth and shifted my chaw and said I was Brawley. Her eyes got big and she bent over and she threw up right there on my shoes.

I have never had anybody throw up on my shoes before and boy was I surprised and just looked at her because I didn't know what to do. But even a slow person like me cares about somebody in trouble but the more I kept tryin' to help her the more she was a-throwin' up until Dug came a-hot-footin' it over and said Brawley close your mouth and go get a mop and bucket and for Godsakes clean your shoes first. So I did what my boss told me to do and he had another lady take the pretty little girl to the bathroom to clean up.

I know why the girl throwed up because Dug told me. I ain't never been called into the office before but one day Dug says Brawley! follow me and I followed him to the office and he tells me to sit in that chair right there and so I did and he proceeds to talk.

Brawley. You might be wonderin' why she threw up on your shoes he says and I says it's because she was sick and Dug says yes she was sick but do you know why she was sick and I shook my head and he says it's because of the chaw. He said Brawley you sure do like your chewin' tobacca and I nodded and he said there were some others whut worked here that liked their chaw too and most folks were used to not lookin' at the big mess that was in those mouths but that this little girl was special.

Brawley he says she ain't never seen a mouthful of swish like you got and being a sensitive person and not knowin' about chaw anyway she naturally got sick and threw up. Naturally I said and Dug said so don't open your mouth around her anymore because she's special and I said she's slow like me and Dug said no, no, no, no. She's ummm well we just want to keep her happy he says and so I weren't to open my mouth around her from this point forward and I said I would not do such anymore and that's a guaranteed fact.

The pretty little girl never asked me for help again. Do not get me wrong. I ain't saying she ain't nice because she is. She'd wave at me from a long ways away but she wouldn't look at me directly and I wasn't mad at her for that because she was special. I do not know what that girl had for dinner before she came to work that night but I do not want to clean that mess off my shoes ever again.

P.V. Rose is a true Georgia Peach, born and raised. She spends her days in a variety of pursuits, some of which you may have heard.

She prefers to remain anonymous in her pursuit as a writer and as such her pen name is an amalgamation of two beloved aunts' names and initials.

The editors of this anthology know who she is and are sworn to secrecy.

Like Gloria Swanson, though, she is ready for her close-up when a Mr. DeMille type calls.

Grave Luck

Michael D. Davis

Fillmore was under the moon in a heat as terrible as a fart that originated from a gas station egg salad sandwich. He walked along the soft grass zigzagging through headstones new and old. Finding Cabott wasn't difficult. He worked by the light of a lamp that flickered and blinked as if giving his location was its sole purpose.

"There ya are," Fillmore said not too loud and not too quiet, just in a tired sort of way.

Still made Cabott jump. "Jesus Christ, you don't sneak up on someone in a graveyard, middle of the night, ya dumb fuck."

"I wasn't sneakin'."

"What the hell else you'd call it?"

Fillmore paused. "Er...*walkin'*?"

"Tryin' to kill me, more like it," Cabott griped. "You get that hole dug?"

"'Course. Been here two hours longer than you. Workin' my ass into a puddle," Fillmore said smugly.

"What do ya want? A medal? It's not like you're gonna get paid overtime."

"It just took me forever."

"Eh, shut up. Just pop the lid, grab the watch, fill the hole."

"That's what I came up 'bout. There was no watch."

Cabott yowled. "What? Impossible. He had it on at visitation. Saw it myself. Expensive thing."

"Well, I looked around and didn't see it. It was sick too cause he's half chewed up and rotted. Hell, he didn't even have no face no more."

"Alright, alright. Just show me."

Fillmore led Cabott over the darkened dead-filled hills to the grave in question. Cabott looked at the headstone and strung together swear words like pearls.

"Fillmore," he said when he finished cussing. "What's the name on the headstone?"

"Billy Devlin."

"Not only is this stone very small and this guy died six months ago, but the name I gave you was *Big Willy* Devlin."

"Oh."

"*Oh?* That's all you got to say," Cabott snarled. "You. Dumb. Sumbitch."

"Well, you don't gotta be mean about it. I got here *early,* in the *dark,* in the *heat,* and by *myself* dug the hole."

"But you dug up the wrong guy. Some poor asshole that probably didn't have a penny to his name livin'. What are we supposed to do with him? Huh? Take his suit and sell it as slightly used?"

"I don't know. Get off my ass."

Cabott snarled. "Eh, shut up. We'll hit the crypts and maybe there'll be a few of those copper vases we can grab. We might make a buck yet. You! Fill the hole."

"Why I gotta?"

"You dug it." Cabott started to walk away when he heard a noise in the distance.

"What's that?"

"My ass breakin'."

"No, goddammit. Someone's comin'. Shit, somethin' flashed."

An old skinny man in a reflective shirt, and shorts that exposed a mile of leg, with a light strapped to his head slowed in front of them.

"What you boys doin' out here?"

"Workin'," Cabott said.

"At three A.M.?"

"Graveyard shift. What are you doin' out?"

"Got myself weak skin. In sun I blister like that. This the only time I can run."

"Well, enjoy."

"Uh huh." The old man started jogging past, giving them one last look. Cabott snatched the shovel and beamed the old man on the head.

Fillmore yelped. "Whatcha do that for?"

"He freaked me out. Talkin' 'bout his skin. Askin' questions. Lookin' at us. We'll lock him in one of the crypts, okay."

Fillmore bent down and checked out the old guy. Then said, "Won't work."

"Why?"

"He's dead."

"Crissakes, can't I catch a break?" Cabott paced around thinking. "Alright, alright. We'll put him in with Billy Devlin."

"Don't think he'll fit in the coffin."

"You. Dumb. Sumbitch. Not in the coffin. On top of it, just in the hole. Cabott shook his head at Fillmore. "And check his pockets."

"What?"

"You heard me. Let's try to make some money. What's he got here? A flip phone? Ten bucks in ones? Anything else? Hey! What's that?"

"Holy fuck. He's wearin' a bracelet over his tube socks."

"What's it made out of?"

"Looks like gold."

"Grab it and let's put him in the damn hole."

It took some doing. Turned out the old guy had a good foot on Mr. Devlin. So, they put him in on his stomach and bent his knees some. It didn't look comfortable, but he wasn't complaining.

Michael D. Davis was born and raised in a small town in Iowa. A high school graduate and avid reader, he has aspired for years to be a writer. He's written over fifty short stories, ranging in genre from comedy to horror and flash fiction to a novella, some of which have been published in Yellow Mama webzine, Out of the Gutter Online, Near to the Knuckle online magazine, Horla, and Sirens Call.

He continues in his accursed pursuit of a career in the written word and, in his hunt, Michael's love for stories in all genres and mediums will not falter.

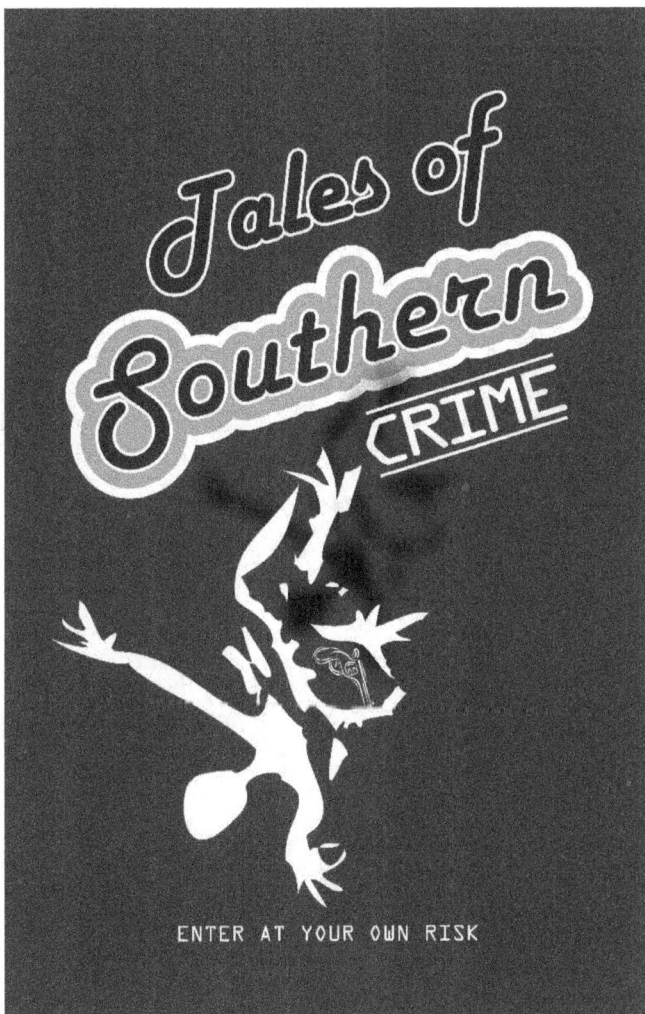

Tales of Southern CRIME

ENTER AT YOUR OWN RISK

THE AUTHORS: CRIME

Gun, No Bullets

Roy Richardson

He handled the heavy little pistol easily, though it was made to fit smaller hands than his. It felt unbalanced, as the barrel was longer than the grip. It was an old chrome-plated, five-shot .38 revolver, with a cute bulldog head molded into either side of the black Bakelite grips. Engraved across the top of the barrel was "Iver Johnson's Arms & Cycle Works Fitchburg, Mass. U.S.A."

With a private smile, he removed the weapon's unnecessary trigger lock. Unnecessary because he kept the gun unloaded, the lock there to keep his girlfriend Francine placated.

Out of old habit, he checked to make sure the pistol was empty of rounds.

The little handgun was modeled after the Smith & Wesson Schofield revolver, the top-break six-shooter popular in the Old West, reportedly used by Bob Ford to back-shoot Jesse James. Though he doubted even that infamous weapon had the dangerous modification this particular handgun sported.

He carefully ran his fingernail along the gun's front sight— a thin, fin-like half circle of metal that some miscreant had honed to razor sharpness. While this dubious modification may have added to the threat potential of the weapon, it hadn't done anything to improve its accuracy.

He'd practiced with the gun, once, before moving to the Big Apple, emptying the five-round chamber without hitting a single one of the Coke cans he was aiming at, disconcerting for someone who considered himself a decent marksman.

Research on the Net quickly told him the fault lay in the weapon, rather than his aim. Referred to as either a "belly gun" or a "suicide pistol", the Iver .38 was known to be notoriously inaccurate, probably due to the cylinder and barrel being misaligned during manufacture, causing the bullets to career off the inside of the barrel rather than being guided by it.

So it wasn't much of a gun, as guns go, but it was what was called in shooter circles a "legacy gun", given to him by his father when he had moved from Atlanta to New York City, the old man thinking that any gun was better than no gun. As such, he knew he'd probably never let it go, due more to sentiment than practicality. He joked to himself that it would probably function best used Wyatt Earp-style, the barrel serving as a chrome-plated club.

He was toying with the pistol as a matter of research. He was a writer of historical novels, and a character in his latest book was destined to do himself in with a .38, so he wanted to get the details right. His readers expected ballistic as well as historical accuracy, and he was determined to give it to them. He'd done his grisly homework via the Net, but there was no stand-in for cold hard steel in your hand.

He broke the gun open, checking yet again to make sure it was indeed unloaded.

His hand shook just a little as, breaking every rule that had been ground into him as a child, he put the barrel of the weapon in his mouth.

Epiphanies jolted him as cool metal touched mucus membranes.

The cold steel partially enveloped by his warm flesh worked on him like a strange drug, producing notions both fearful and revelatory.

Like the ancient Apaches who'd consumed mescaline concoctions to aid them in their spirit quests, he supped deeply from the primal truths of the Gun of the Hand.

Thoughts random yet related strafed his consciousness, leaving impressions of unity, but evading cohesion.

William Shatner's voice sprang clearly into his racing brain, wrenched unbid from the massive and complex tangle of synapses, neurons, and minute electromagnetic impulses that were "him". He smiled around the gun barrel, an experience as enlightening as it was bizarre. The fictional Captain Kirk had long served as a wonky bellwether in his life's journey and functioned now as an oddly pacifying voice: "How we face death is at least as important as how we face life."

Just approaching middle age, he had never truly faced his own mortality, or seriously considered ending his own existence. Oh, there had of course been the juvenile dabbling spawned from adolescent angst ("They'll see! They'll be sorry!"), but he'd come through that fire as all but the most desperate do.

His parents, though old, were both still alive and in good health, as were his siblings, close relatives, and friends. Yes, he'd lost a few acquaintances to tragedy along the way, but their passing had either been utterly random, or caused by their own foolish actions, and so were easily reconciled by his indoctrinated Belief System, in this case Protestantism of the Southern Baptist variety, filtered, mutated, and seasoned by a lifetime of exposure to, among myriad other influences, "Star Trek", Buddhism, and the raw, blunt stupidity of his fellow man.

But what if all that — all the thoughts, experiences, kindnesses, hard-won wisdom, and extravagant foolishnesses alike; all of the pieces of reality that went into making the one unique "him" — were to suddenly end, on a whim, in the bat of an eye, with the pull of an uncaring trigger?

An unusual clarity took hold of him, a certainty of thought experienced in short bursts by only a tiny fraction of humanity, usually cut short unrecorded by firing squads, the gallows, or upended bottles of prescription pharmaceuticals.

Just as he desperately grasped at this elusive cosmic truth, the door behind him clicked open.

It was his live-in girlfriend, the witty, urbane, and gun-hating Francine, of Tarrytown, New York.

* * * * *

He and Frannie were sophisticated, well-spoken creatives who mingled well at parties, drank martinis, had every episode of "Mad Men" on DVD, and made a good living from their talents. His Cracker upbringing gave him just enough of an edge to make him interesting to the fickle creatures known as the New York Intelligentsia. Until he fucked up and talked about firearms, a mistake he quickly learned to avoid.

As were most born in the South, he had been raised around guns and, while he respected them, he did not fear them unless they were pointed at him. This made him a rare breed in New York City: a law-abiding citizen who was actually comfortable around guns. It was not a breed that was popular with the NYC Cognoscenti, a group of which Frannie counted herself a proud member.

Frannie had never held a gun of any sort, had rarely even seen a firearm in real life, aside from the rusting shotgun that collected dust on her grandfather's mantle, an aged chunk of metal and wood she considered more an *objet d'art* than an actual weapon. To Francine, and indeed to millions of her fellow New Yorkers, guns, when thought of at all, were seen as either plot devices in popular entertainments, or as objects of necessary evil when borne by soldiers and policemen, things of pure malevolence when wielded by anyone else.

Sane people did not touch them, much less own them.

In the South, the fact that he owned only one pistol, and did not carry it on his person or in his car, caused some to look at him as a bit effeminate.

In the North, this exact same circumstance resulted in him labeled a hopeless Neanderthal.

He was generally amused by both judgments.

Being a student of history as well as a keen observer of human nature, he understood where and why these two opposing viewpoints originated. To his chagrin, he could relate to both sides. He had grown up among the clannish descendants of government-hating English and Scots Irish who'd fled their countries to escape the domineering British aristocracy, and who had tamed their wild new homeland with grit, determination, and the ubiquitous musket.

The ensuing centuries had done little to temper the bellicose natures of people who considered themselves the spiritual heirs of Daniel Boone, Davy Crockett, and the honorable Robert E. Lee. To these folks, the firearm was no less than an Instrument of Destiny, bequeathed unto them by John Browning, Samuel Colt, and the Good Lord Almighty Himself and enshrined as sacred by the Second Amendment. Never mind that it was the gubmint they railed against that had done the enshrining.

On the flipside were his New York neighbors, folks considered by his Southern kin to be Johnny-Come-Lately Americans at best, as many of their descendants had come over well after what most hill folk considered the defining event of their history, the War of Northern Aggression. By their lights, if you didn't have people in that fight, on one side or the other, well, you just didn't have a place at the table in American politics, and you sure as sin had no say whatsoever in how real Americans lived their lives.

Naturally, Yankees, and New Yorkers in particular, did not cotton to this way of looking at things. The Civil War being ancient history, it was an event of little concern to them save that the right folks got their asses kicked and slaves got their freedom. All else was an unhealthy sort of ancestor worship.

Their concerns had been shaped by history of a much more recent vintage. Guns, wars, and armies clad in gray had entirely different meanings to these Americans. To them, firearms were not instruments of freedom, but rather tools used to promote pogroms, holocaust, and genocide. To them, more guns in no way implied more freedom.

The irony was, of course, that both sides had much in common. Both sides' attitudes had been born out of manmade cataclysms of blood and steel. Both sides were equally determined that this fate would never befall them and theirs again.

Neither side was willing to compromise. Neither side understood the concepts of Yin/Yang, of the interplay of black, white, and gray, of the natural rhythm of the universe, which, violent as it could be, always swung back toward the middle, toward balance.

Absolutist philosophies breed absolutist solutions. That which will not bend will eventually break. Nature abhors a stubborn asshole almost as much as a vacuum.

The animal instinct for survival at any cost must be tempered by compromise and rational thought, else humankind would never be anything but very clever killer apes, pounding away at one another ceaselessly and pointlessly.

He had put the gun in his pocket once or twice, when walking the streets of New York City late at night, trying to break a bout of writer's block. Having the pistol on his person had made him feel safe, powerful, godlike, even an arbiter of life and death. But then he realized what he was doing: looking at every person he met as someone he might have to shoot. It was not a mindset he wanted to be saddled with.

When he got back to his apartment, he put the gun away, and never carried it again.

This reality was what seemed to evade open-carry advocates: When you carry a firearm, you are not automatically safer, smarter, or more qualified to make decisions of life and death. But you are instantly responsible for every single human being within the range of that weapon, not just the people you might possibly protect, but also the ones you might not, the ones you might fail to save, or God forbid, accidentally shoot.

This was not a burden he, or most people, were equipped to bear.

All this he glimpsed, and grasped at, and sought to comprehend as a tangible whole, as he sat alone in the Brooklyn apartment he shared with Francine, tasting the gun.

* * * * *

Frannie shrieked like a scream queen in a horror movie.

In his haste to remove the gun from his mouth, he sliced his lip with the sharpened front sight. All the mighty revelations ringing in his brain fled back into his subconscious like sweet dreams banished by the tyranny of an unrelenting alarm clock. A trickle of blood ran down his chin and dripped onto his hand. Frannie screamed again when she saw the thin stream of scarlet.

"Frannie, goddammit, stop that takin' on!" His Southern speech patterns emerged when he was stressed. "What are you doin' home, anyway?"

Frannie's eyes bulged, her voice shrill. "What am I doing? What am *I* doing? What the fuck are *you* doing?" She pointed with a shaking hand to the bloodied pistol he still held.

Rattled by Frannie's cries and demeanor, and conscious of the revelations that fled his seeking mind, he struggled to remain calm. "Honey, it's not what you think, I'm doing research. Look, it's not even loaded."

He worked the release mechanism on top of the gun with his bloody hand, showed her the empty cylinder. But all erudite and sophisticated Francine, of Tarrytown, New York, saw were two things — blood and guns. Things known in psychiatric circles as, ironically enough, triggers.

From deep beneath her liberal logic and Vassar education, simian impulses took hold of her.

He knew that Frannie's mother had been mentally ill and verbally abusive, and had finally committed suicide when Frannie was twelve, not with a gun, but by slitting her wrists. But what he didn't know, what Francine had never told him, was that she had found her mother's body floating in the blood-filled tub, that she had screamed and screamed until someone called the police, police who came with their bland words and heavy tread, and guns — guns and blood, enough of both to last Francine a lifetime.

Rather than quieting her, the sight of the bloody gun caused her to scream yet again.

She surprised him by lunging for it, her only thought to get it out of sight, to throw it into the garbage, or out the window.

Had he just let her have the gun, the situation would have been defused. But putting a gun, even an unloaded one, into the hands of an irrational person went against his every instinct. And so he struggled to keep the pistol from her.

Both became slippery with crimson as they wrestled for the gun, the sharpened sight slashing their hands. Not understanding where the cuts were coming from made Frannie become utterly unhinged. Caterwauling like a dying animal, she yanked on the gun with all her strength, then, at his greatest point of resistance, she shoved it in the opposite direction, toward him, striking him in the face with the barrel.

As is the case with any hard, angular object wielded in anger by a human being, the gun became a force multiplier, far more dangerous than any fleshy hand or fist.

Her accidental strike partially severed his right eyelid, spraying them with more blood. He released the pistol. Francine shook the hand grasping the gun as though to rid herself of a poisonous snake yet could not make her clenched fist open to release it.

They paused, she stunned by the result of her unthinking blow, he by the force of it, and the sight of so much of his own bright, shiny life fluid staining them both.

It might have ended there, had his shock and pain not been replaced with animal anger. Monkey logic took over. Pain inflicted creates the desire to reciprocate in kind.

"You crazy-ass Yankee bitch!"

This seemingly generic insult would have left her unfazed coming from a stranger, but coming from the man who should have known her better than anyone else on earth it cut deep. She switched gears from crazed to furious in an instant.

"How dare you, you...you...white trash redneck!"

Mutually assured destruction reared its ugly head. He'd been called worse by other snobby New Yorkers, but never by her. He rarely lost his temper, but when he did, the loss was absolute.

He backhanded her clumsily with his left hand, his right being occupied with staunching the flow of his life's blood. He had never raised his hand to her before; she had in fact only been struck thus once in her entire life, as a child by her mother.

More old wounds were reopened, more triggers pulled. Mindless fury flamed within her.

Things had been unleashed in them that modern humans rarely experience outside of warfare, things they were not equipped by training or experience to handle.

Nature took over. Fight or flight kicked in. Thousands of years of civilized behavior temporarily went out the window.

She had bloodied him.

He would do the same to her.

He became her mother, whom she had always wanted to repay for her cruelty. She thought briefly of running, as she had run from her demented parent her entire life, but he was between her and the door.

Flight was replaced by Fight.

He lunged at her, screaming wordlessly, and she hit him again with the gun. It was an awkward blow, producing more pain than damage.

The furious chimpanzee he had become struck her in the face with all his might. She fell back, her head impacting the sharp corner of his desk. She momentarily lost consciousness, as bleeds that would soon kill her bloomed in her brain.

The sight of her limp, drooling form satiated the killer chimp within him. He bent over her, desperately calling her name.

Adrenaline shot through her as her body sensed his animal nearness. Her eyes opened to see the bloody, maimed creature who'd murdered her looming. Instinctually, she lashed out with the gun still gripped in her shock-clenched hand.

The razor-sharp sight slashed his carotid artery wide open. His warm life's blood poured over her.

Horrified, she lapsed back into unconsciousness for the final time as his heart rhythmically pumped his life away. He managed to dial 911 before passing out.

* * * * *

Under "Cause of Death" the reporting officer wrote factually and utterly without irony —

"Gun, no bullets."

Writer/artist Roy Richardson hasn't had a real job in over thirty years, except for four years of teaching, which proved to be a mistake.

He and his wife currently illustrate the long-running syndicated comic strip "Mary Worth". That leaves him one day a week for writing — if he keeps up with his deadlines.

facebook.com/hillbilliespreferblondes/

Ice in Her Veins

Patricia Bowen

Reprinted from
Unintended Consequences: Collected Stories

No use lyin'. They got me. Thought I was the hottest thing in town, but now I see I might not be. Just might not. Tell ya how it happened, one step at a time.

I was bundled up, had the heater in my pickup cranked to high but it was barely keepin' the snow and sleet melted off the windshield. It was like I was drivin' through a long white tunnel, and the ice here and there on the road was hard to see 'cause it wasn't light out yet. Daddy always said I was headstrong, and he was right. I had to get in and out of where I was goin' before dawn so I could have my alibi, and bad weather or not I was on my way to get the job done.

Takin' the curve faster than I should've, almost hit this kid on the side of the road with his thumb out and looking like he was wearin' everything he owned 'cept what was in the backpack on his shoulder. Not a good idea for me to stop, but geez, what were his odds of a lift at 4 AM on a Sunday morning? Slim to none. And, thinkin' back, I was the stupid, sorry slim.

"Hey, man. Hop in."

"Thank you, ma'am. Thought I was going to freeze out there."

A little young for my taste, but I wasn't plannin' on marryin' him. I just didn't want him to slow me down this trip. "What's your name and where're ya' goin'?"

"Carter. Carter James, ma'am. Got me a job in Canton, and with this weather and all thought I'd set out early so I don't miss my first day. How about you?"

"Well, Carter James, I'm Shelly Lewis and I'm on my way to work at The Roadside, early shift waitress, but I don't think we'll be havin' too much of a breakfast crowd this mornin'."

We talked back and forth a bit, mostly 'bout the cold. When I told him I'd have to drop him off halfway, he said, "That's okay. I'll go with you to the restaurant. I could use a meal and might pick up another ride there."

Ding, ding. The bells went off in my head. He didn't have no job. His story wasn't any truer than mine. "You won't get no other ride in this storm. Come clean with me, Carter. What were you really doin' out on Highway 9?"

"Didn't mean to lie to you, Ms. Lewis. My foster people put me out last night. I just turned eighteen and they won't get the monthly check for me anymore, so they gave me fifty dollars and told me to catch a bus to someplace warm. They were up to no good and didn't want me around. Thought I was too smart for my own good. I swear that's the true story."

"Well, since you're comin' clean with me and you got no place else to go, I'll tell you my true story if you promise to keep it to yourself. Promise?"

"Sure. I promise."

"Okay. My man doesn't know I know he's been runnin' around with another woman. He's a trucker, and instead of bein' out of town on the road like he told me he was, he's been shackin' up at her place. I'm on my way to her trailer to catch them together and shake up their little love nest. Wanna come and see the show?"

"I...I guess so. Nothing better to do, and you might need some help, some protection."

Seemed like a good idea at the time, bringin' the boy along. But when we got to the tramp's place and saw my cheater's truck cab parked on the side, I wasn't so sure. Carter tried to talk me out of goin' in, thought it might be dangerous. Told me he'd seen enough violence in the places he'd lived and he was afraid. Well, I didn't come all this way to hear that.

I took Daddy's six-shot Colt from my pocket and destroyed the lock on her door. Walked in with Carter behind me, his mouth gapin' like a bass. The happy couple in the bed didn't look so happy right then. I put one right between her eyes, so he could watch it happen, and then I gave him one and the same. Lord, I saved my reputation.

Carter screamed — I didn't know men screamed — and pulled my arm back so fast the gun went off in his face, right under his left eye.

Nothing more to do there, so I put the gun in Carter's hand and went out to my pickup. I rummaged through his backpack on the seat, took out the fifty. He wasn't lyin' about that. I went back to the trailer and put the backpack next to his body. The snow had stopped and the sky was gettin' pink. Time to go.

I got to church just in time to slip in behind the lectern. Feelin' generous, I dropped the fifty in the collection plate, a foolish move on my part 'cause it got me some attention I didn't need and turned out to be counterfeit. Yeah, Carter's foster people were up to no good all right.

Patricia Bowen spent 35 years in sales, marketing, international business development, and training and coaching with large multinational companies. She currently donates her time and services to various programs for women, senior citizens, and the mentally disabled population in local communities.

Four years ago she began trying her hand at fiction in short stories and novellas, mostly about strong women with complicated lives. She has proudly appeared in the *Table for Two* anthology, The Sun magazine, and earned honorable mentions in various contests. Her two recent books of fiction are *The Cure* and *Unintended Consequences: Collected Stories* (which includes this short story) and are available on Amazon.com.

patriciabowen.com
Facebook.com/WoodsgalWrites
Twitter @WoodsgalWrites
amazon.com/author/patriciaannbowen

Nashville Nights

Sean Liam Hastings

November 2009

Nashville was one of those places in the South where the old and new blended together into something found only in that one spot. Red-brick buildings, darkened by years of wear and weather and advertising live country music and BBQ via neon signs, stood guard over the old Nashville in front of the tallest building in the entire State of Tennessee — a thirty three story skyscraper with AT&T's logo at the very top. The two towers that rose over its logo, like a pair of cropped ears, and darkened glass windows were why some locals called it the Batman Building.

Scott Larson saw all that from a window in the office rented by his soon-to-be new employer, a private investigator named Mark Laurent. Mark was a thin man of moderate height, just a few inches shorter than Scott. He had light-brown skin that gave Scott the impression he was biracial. A country baritone meant he could get around most of the region without drawing too much attention.

"What is it that leads a fellow to resign from the CIA, then pack his bags and move here?" Mark asked. He was at his desk. Scott occupied a chair on the opposite side.

"Wasn't what I wanted to do with my life," the latter replied. "I'm pushing thirty years old and I want to turn this dream of mine into reality."

"I admire a man who goes after what he wants. And Marines always make good workers, even the shit ones."

During their first phone conversation Mark had told Scott that he served in the Navy. He even talked like a sailor, with more saltiness than most Southerners. The bio on his company website mentioned his military background and later career in the Naval Criminal Investigative Service. He assigned Scott his first job: Organize the office. Which was a hell of a lot easier said than done. Stacks of papers with dates from the last century occupied the corner now designated Scott's workspace. Every file in the large, rusted metal drawers had a different system of organization.

Mark explained that this was a consequence of employees being hired and leaving shortly thereafter multiple times, over the last decade. "I hope this time will be different," he told Scott.

Mark went over what the next six months were going to look like for Scott. He was technically an apprentice private investigator, thanks to a written notice from Mark to the State government. Half a year of on-the-job training would precede the exam for a State license, with sixteen hours of continuing education every year afterward. The first half of a private investigator's education went into technique, the second went into an understanding of the laws that regulated their job.

Mark left the office at 11:30 to pick up a couple of sandwiches for them. He returned at 12:30; the line was long at The Row but the food was well worth the wait. His jaw dropped when he saw what Scott had already accomplished. Most people would have taken an entire day to do half that much; most veterans would have probably finished at 3:00.

Fuckin' Marines.

The few, the proud, the overzealous.

That afternoon Mark brought Scott out with him on a stakeout. They waited in Mark's car down the block from an overpriced restaurant while the experienced private investigator, the apprentice's master, prepared an expensive camera for shots taken at long range.

"The man we're waiting on is in the process of divorcing an artist you'll hear every now and then on country radio stations," Mark explained. "He's claiming his wife was the primary breadwinner and that he's entitled to spousal support."

A limousine arrived. Mark aimed the camera. A man in his forties, wearing a bespoke designer shirt that must have cost upwards of a thousand bucks, got out and held the door for two college-aged women in dresses that met the bare minimum of private coverage. The man had an arm around each as they walked to the restaurant entrance.

"Good luck with your settlement, shithead," Mark muttered. The camera made sharp clicks as the hunter took snapshots of his prey.

Later, they closed the office. Mark invited his new employee out to a nearby bar. Out of friendliness and a desire to learn more about his new city, Scott accepted. There were far worse ways to end a first day on the job than getting a beer with the boss.

"What'd you do in the Navy?" Scott asked over the din of a crowd and music coming from a stage at the front near the street.

"I was a special boat crewman," Mark replied, then sucked the foam off the top of the glass.

"SWCC?" It was pronounced *swick*.

"Yep. Our job was to infil operators for a job and exfil them once it was done or rescue them if something went wrong."

"Then NCIS?"

Mark took a long sip of his beer. "It wasn't like what you see in the TV show. Nobody ever slapped me in the back of the head. At least, nobody that wanted to keep their hand. It was more often a boring drug case than something dramatic like a murder. I liked investigating, I liked a lot of things about that job, but I hated the bureaucracy. Government red tape here, there, and everywhere. Going off on my own helped me even out... ummm, you know, the parts of my work that I liked with the parts I didn't."

Scott nodded. His story was similar, though he doubted Mark had ever been in a rooftop fistfight with a spy-turned-jihadist from Qatar. But that was a story for another time.

Mark talked a little about growing up in Nashville and leaving NCIS when his father got sick. "So...what made you go down this path?"

"Well..." Scott meandered. "It's...it's something I've always been attracted to. I always read detective stories when I was a kid. At a certain point, I started to be able to piece together the mystery before the characters. Even when I was in the military or other lines of work, I always wondered what this job would be like."

"Even when you were CIA?"

Scott instinctively looked around.

"I take it there's not much you're allowed to say about that," Mark said.

"You'd be correct. But I'll say this much: When I became a Marine, we were told 'you have spent your entire lives waiting for this moment, waiting to be born!' Ever since I left Active Duty, I've been waiting to be reborn. I hoped the Agency would be it, but it just wasn't. Now I want to try something I've spent my entire life wanting to do."

Mark nodded but was soon checking out a group of young women sitting at the other end of the bar. "That's a hell of a story," he muttered. "Hey, wanna be my wingman or fly solo tonight?"

Scott looked at the group Mark was glancing at. "Nah, not tonight."

"No?"

"Not what I'm looking for...at the moment."

Scott left out the fact he was in the middle of a divorce and that he was living in a single-room occupancy on the eastern side of the city. Not the sort of place for long-term romance or even a short fling. This was a temporary period of transition that would end once he got his P.I. license and the lawyers finalized everything with his soon-to-be ex-wife.

"Alright. See you tomorrow morning." Mark was already on his way to the group. He said something that made them all laugh and took a seat nearby. Despite his workplace reticence, Mark could certainly be the life of a party when he wanted to.

As Scott took note of that, he also noticed a drunken customer about to collide with a distracted waitress holding a tray full of drinks in one hand. He got up on instinct and moved close to intervene but arrived too late. The man bumped into the woman. A beer on the tray fell and would have landed in someone's plate if Scott had not caught it. Frothy alcohol spilled across the table but neither the glass nor adjacent plates shattered. The women at the table looked up, recognized the near-miss, and gave each other a "holy shit" look.

The drunk shuffled away. The waitress apologized profusely. Scott looked around the room before he gave the fallen glass back to the server. He was about to walk away when someone from the table asked, "How did you do that?"

She was African-American, with natural hair and curves that briefly distracted him from everything else.

"Saw it coming," Scott replied.

"Well, thank you for that," she said. "I think you've earned a spot with us. I'm Brianna."

Scott sat, introduced himself, and learned their names. But Brianna was the one who really interested him. He ordered another drink and an entrée she recommended before the group started asking him questions.

"What do you do?"

"Just had my first day on the job."

"What's that?"

"I guess you could say private investigator."

"You guess?"

"I'm very new at it. Very green."

"What'd you do before that?"

"Had a job in the federal government. It was unfulfilling, didn't pay well. I got tired of it."

"What did you do?" Brianna asked.

I was an operations officer in the CIA's Counterintelligence Center, Scott almost replied. Instead, he stuck to his boring pencil-pusher story — which was a more honest depiction of the typical Agency career than most people would assume. When they all decided it was time to go home for the worknight, Scott paid for his meal and exchanged phone numbers with Brianna.

January 2010

The next three months were a time of structured learning and free-flowing exploration for Scott Larson. Mark Laurent gradually taught him the basics of private investigation, a job where careful planning and in-the-moment improvising went together seamlessly. There were some skills, such as surveillance and self-defense, Scott already had a good grasp on. Mark commented that ex-cops and military veterans tended to roll in loud and proud, broadcasting themselves to the target. Private investigators needed to remain unnoticed in order to get the job done.

The part that Scott was least familiar with were the rules and regulations pertaining to the job. Law enforcement and intelligence officers had a lot more leeway than some random, albeit certified, private citizen being hired for a job by another private citizen. Breaking and entering, blackmail, or unwarranted physical altercations would result in one's license being stripped. Scott had to learn what not to do before he could accompany Mark on the streets. With proper permits private investigators were allowed to carry firearms for self-defense, but Mark refused to do so himself.

"Those who live by the gun die by it, usually from their own gun," he said, sitting at his desk while Scott organized current case files. Mark then opened a drawer and pulled out a KA-BAR knife. "Besides, I get by just fine with this."

After saving up multiple paychecks, Scott had enough cash to buy a pistol. A gun show in Murfreesboro provided a golden opportunity to acquire weapons. For self-defense, of course; he heard gunshots in his neighborhood every now and again. Scott had no idea how lenient Tennessee's gun laws were until he arrived at the firearms flea market. With no background check necessary — although he would have passed one just fine — he purchased a Beretta M9 semiautomatic and a Smith & Wesson Model 625 revolver for much lower prices than anticipated.

Scott spent his off-hours working out. Past marital stress and a CIA desk job were part of the reason why he had gotten out of shape. Reading books purchased on sale and being shown parts of Nashville by Brianna also took up his time. Locals always had a better grasp of a place than paid tour guides. She showed him various open-mic clubs where prospective singers could try their luck. She went up every time and was always one of the best. Scott never accepted her dare to go up after her. It made sense when she told him that her corporate gig paid well but left her unfulfilled. Making music was what she wished she could do for a living. Scott had a feeling she could go far in that industry.

He was less sure about what may or may not happen between them. The signals she gave him ranged from seemingly interested to neutral but friendly. And he had not yet decided whether he was here to stay or if he would move to another city once his apprenticeship was over.

In addition to open-mics, they got lunch at the Butchertown Hall in the Historic Germantown District, sipped whiskey at Nelson's Green Briar Distillery, and — good Lord — visited a full-scale model of the Parthenon located two miles west of downtown.

"They used to call Nashville 'the Athens of the South'," Brianna explained. "That's why they built the replica here."

"I think Athens, Georgia, would dispute that title," Scott replied.

February 2010

By February, Scott spent a majority of his work hours away from his desk. Office supply errands graduated to visiting archives looking for evidence, then on-foot and vehicular surveillance operations. His previous training at The Farm and experience working at the CIA's London Station served him well during these assignments.

The first case involved Scott and Mark tag-teaming to watch a middle-aged man accused of faking the grievous shoulder injury that prompted his monthly disability checks. The target lived in a suburb where parking on the street was illegal; they would have to pose as pedestrians in order to keep an eye on his house. Scott suggested they wear a different set of clothes each time one of them passed it; this would lessen the chance of the target or his neighbors recognizing them and getting suspicious.

Five hours in, Scott was walking by the house when their target emerged carrying a mountain bike over his shoulders. Scott took out a small digital camera — though larger and more conspicuous than the ones his former co-workers used — and discreetly accomplished the mission to collect damning evidence.

It was the most satisfying work Scott had done since returning from London.

Another time involved watching a motel parking lot for evidence of illegal activities. They were working for a personal injury law firm suing the premises for negligent security. Months earlier their client had been shot in the parking lot and barely survived. Scott knew his complexion made him stand out in the neighborhood but he played well the part of someone down on his luck and got photographs of a drug deal. The lawyers wrangled a large settlement for their client, which led to them recommending Scott and Mark to other law firms in Nashville.

That was how they ended up on the trail of a steroid-abusing deadbeat father. They found someone they considered a likely suspect. Mark wanted to confirm by following him on foot. Their target was described as a bodybuilder turned professional leg breaker for local loan sharks. Six-foot-five and covered head to toe in an unnatural amount of muscle. Scott wanted to share some Agency tradecraft to lessen the risks that the target would spot them but deferred to Mark's judgment this time.

Big mistake.

Mark found himself in an alley pressed up against a wall by the roid-raging behemoth. Scott ran at top speed, jumped, and put the target in a headlock. His feet were dangling off the ground as the wannabe Mr. Universe moved backward and slammed Scott into a wall. Scott grunted loudly but maintained his grip long enough to initiate a blood choke, or sleeper hold. The target lunged backward into the wall a second time and Scott let out a big *oooof.* The only thought in Scott's mind was to maintain his grip.

Maintain.

At all costs!

The target initiated his third attempt but collapsed before he reached the wall. When Mr. Universe hit the ground Scott released his grip and realized he too could not breathe. The wind was just knocked out of him. Not his first time. He stayed calm as his diaphragm went back to normal and oxygen started reaching his lungs again.

"You okay?" Mark rasped.

"Y-yeah," Scott rasped back.

Mark nodded. "Thanks, man. Holy shit."

Next time, I'm speaking my mind, Scott said to himself. If I see a bad plan, I'll say so.

Even with long stretches of boredom and occasional moments of peril, Scott found he loved this job. Mark gave him more autonomy than any boss he had worked for in the military or the Agency. On top of that, he was going to places and walking the streets instead of being chained to his desk from opening to closing. His new job had almost everything he liked about his previous careers without the parts he had come to hate. On his off hours, Scott continued to hang out with Brianna and watch her sing in open-mic clubs.

He had expected Nashville to be a temporary period of transition for him. He thought in the beginning he would move to Texas or Georgia or maybe just drift around the South before settling on a final locale. But he was also in no hurry to leave; he felt like he had freedom in this city, freedom the likes of which he had longed for back when he lived in Fairfax County, Virginia. This expansion of his horizons came at the cost of no longer hunting enemy intelligence operations and coincided with his divorce, but freedom never came for free. Even though he could now afford a one-bedroom apartment, Scott remained in his single-room occupancy to save cash for the future.

March 2010

By March, when spring was threatening to thaw winter's chill, Scott was preparing for the State exam required for his license. He was never one to leave studying to the last minute; he did this on his breaks from assisting Mark on stakeouts or unrolling dusty archives in the local records departments. On the second Wednesday, Mark briefed Scott on an unusual and highly-lucrative assignment.

They were going to drive out into nearby farmland around 3:00 AM to watch another target. This woman, who received monthly disability checks, was said to be doing hard manual labor in her barn. Their job was to watch the target and gather photographic evidence if the allegations were true. No matter the hardships or danger, Scott was always excited for something like this.

They took Scott's pickup truck down a high-beam-illuminated dirt road after the two had gotten a few hours of sleep and a cup of coffee. Mark vetoed bringing energy drinks on the grounds that taking a leak could result in the target spotting them. They parked on land owned by someone Mark knew and walked a few miles through the dark woods. Pine needles scratched their faces. Scott tripped on a root. It had been a long while since either man had done something like this; unlike now, they had night-vison goggles on those times.

They took up a position behind a fallen log once they reached the target's house. A gap between the ground and rotting wood allowed just enough space for their cameras. Scott pulled a camouflage tarp from his backpack and set it up for concealment as well as rain protection for their gear. Mark sprayed himself and Scott with a scent-blocker used by deer hunters. Shortly, lights turned on inside the target's home. Soon the door opened; a large animal covered in dark fur sprinted out.

The dog ran around the backyard in circles before stomping straight toward Mark and Scott's log. *Oh fuck,* the latter said to himself as the Rottweiler stopped to sniff the ground. Both men were silent while Mark got his KA-BAR ready. The dog walked up to the fallen tree and lifted her leg. They shifted their cameras up to protect them from the stream and acrid-smelling puddle that resulted. Someone's voice, probably the target's, boomed in the distance and the dog instantly started running back to the house.

"Shit," Scott muttered.

"We're lucky it didn't come to that," Mark replied. "Told you the spray works."

Over the next three hours the sun rose. Their target walked outside with the dog following closely. She was fifty seven years old and had inherited this property from a relative. This supposedly-disabled individual managed to carry boxes about as large as herself to her barn, chores the two private investigators documented with pictures and video.

They packed up around 8:00 AM and treaded back the path they had stomped hours earlier. But the path looked quite different in the daylight. Everything seemed fine until, miles later, they were finally one farm away from the property where they had parked. Scott looked around out of habit and an abundance of caution. That was how he noticed a young man in his twenties with his arms tied behind his back and an elderly woman following him.

Scott stopped in his tracks and muttered, "What the hell?"

The two pairs of people were far enough apart that one was barely visible to the other. Scott squinted and noticed the old woman had a handgun pointed at the young man's back as she marched him to God-knows-where.

"You see that?" Scott asked. "We've got to call the cops."

"Yeah…" Mark hesitated. "I don't know if that's the best idea."

"What do you mean?"

"Look…I know that lady. There's a certain way things are done in these parts and she's old-fashioned, in that sense. Whatever that is, it's a local thing."

"She's got a young fella held at gunpoint and you're saying we ought to just do nothing?"

"It's the way things are done out here."

"What in the hell are you—"

"Scott, that gun probably isn't even loaded," Mark interrupted.

"Probably?"

"Look, I know that woman. I don't know him, but I know her. She's just going to put the fear of God in him and let him go. Catch and release. I know her; she does this from time to time."

Scott's brow furrowed and his jaw hung open. "Man, I...I can't just look the other way on this."

"I know it sounds...fucked up. But that's just the way it is around here. This doesn't happen in the city, but we're not in the city. This is the Old South, what's left of it."

Scott looked down. "This is..." He looked back up. "What we're doing is wrong. It just is."

"Yeah," Mark replied. "But it's also the way it is. I'd change it if I could; I learned the hard way that I can't. We can't. It's just is the way it is."

Scott sighed. "Okay."

His mentor nodded. "Now, let's get the flying fuck out of these woods."

* * * * *

A couple days later on a Sunday morning, Scott opened his laptop to catch up on the previous week's news. He intended to scroll down some sites he followed and spend the rest of his day off studying for the State's exam, but then he noticed a face he recognized. He clicked on an article titled "Missing Man Found Dead of Opioid Overdose", squinted, and confirmed that the man in the picture was the hostage he had seen days earlier. The article said that twenty-three-year-old Hiram Parry had been reported missing days earlier and was found on the side of a dirt road the night before. Investigators believed he had spent days moving on foot from town to town shortly before his accidental overdose. The article said Parry had a record for drug possession and distribution.

Scott's blood ran cold as he thought about what he could have done to prevent this. He had been right there, literally walked past a chance to save the young man's life. Accidental overdose, his ass. Hiram Parry had been kidnapped and most likely murdered; surely forensics would pick that up.

Would they? Or would they go with Occam's Razor and move on to something more pressing than the death of a degenerate? Scott would not be able to live with himself if it came to that.

He walked out to his pickup and drove through the city to the nearest police station. He parked and approached a front desk divided from the incomers by bullet-resistant glass. He identified himself, stated his business, and spent half an hour sitting as he waited for a Lieutenant Wilson. A forty-something man in a cheap dress shirt and khakis, with a glistening badge on his hip, emerged from the Authorized Personnel Only door.

"Mr. Larson," he said. "Please follow me."

Scott was surprised when the plainclothes investigator led him out to the parking lot instead of deeper into the station. Wilson listened as Scott explained the situation. Wilson started asking questions over the sound of vehicles speeding past them. The first two or three were about Hiram Parry but the following focused on Scott and Mark. He remembered what Mark said about legality and liability, so he chose his words carefully. Scott wondered if he was now a suspect; but if that were the case, why had Lieutenant Wilson brought him outside instead of into an interrogation room?

"Well, Mr. Larson, your cooperation is appreciated. I'll have people look into this," the detective said before extending his hand. "If you come across something new or remember something from that morning, give me a call."

Scott shook his hand and took a card with a sergeant's contact information. His heart started beating faster when Wilson turned around and walked back into the station.

What the hell had he just done? What did it accomplish? Most importantly of all, why did Wilson want to keep this between the two of them and not involve other cops?

Over the next five days, Scott forced himself to feign the trust he had gradually built with Mark. First, Mark admitted knowing the woman who held Hiram Parry at gunpoint. Then, Mark had prevented him from calling the cops about it. Finally, when he went to the police by himself, Wilson isolated him and sent him on his way.

Something was rotten about this situation. Rotten to the core.

Scott tapped into his counterintelligence background to a degree unprecedented since his departure from the Agency. If for no other reason than to prevent Mark from becoming suspicious, he put on a friendly face and continued to work hard despite his growing distrust of him. Scott needed his adversaries, whoever they were, to remain in the dark until he managed to pull himself out.

He finally managed to relax a little when he went out with Brianna that Friday night. They both had a couple of drinks at an open-mic club before Brianna went up on stage. She kicked ass, as Scott expected she would, before she returned to their table amid claps from patrons and staff alike. They ordered a third round and talked for a while before they ordered a fourth. He felt a conflicting range of emotions as their evening together drew to a close.

Brianna was the first woman Scott had gone out with since his divorce and it was clear he had no idea what he was doing. Sometimes her presence distracted him from everything else; sometimes she unintentionally made him think about his ex-wife. He thought about how great things had been in the beginning, how stressful it had been when he was being deployed, how painful it was when they tried and failed to start a family, then the constant fighting that defined the final chapter of their relationship. Sometimes Brianna seemed interested in him and sometimes not. Scott's assessment was that they both felt conflicted about the other. Made sense given his current career limbo and her aspirations of escaping the corporate world to sing on stage. There was some instinctual part of their brains trying to pull them together, a component of the mind that rebelled against occupational logic.

Scott nearly summoned the guts to try for a kiss before she got into a taxi but ultimately held back. The likelihood of doing something irreparably stupid in his current state of minor intoxication was too high. They hugged before she got in the cab and he started walking back to his place. His mind was still occupied by her long after they parted ways. Whatever sexual spark existed between them was probably just that. If she did want him, most likely she only had something casual in mind.

But one-night stands and short-term flings were not Scott's thing. He preferred to get to know someone before getting naked with them; after that, he preferred to only get naked with that one person. It became harder for him to deny that neither of them was ready for the other. She did not want to get tied down and there was no way in hell he could maintain a relationship at the moment. He felt something strange, almost like a stab in the gut, as he focused on the fact that neither he nor Brianna were ready.

It was only a few seconds after this realization that Scott paused at a crosswalk, looked around as he waited for the lights to change, and saw two men from the restaurant approaching him from thirty yards away. Shit, he had been careless. Too distracted by liquor and unfulfilled attraction to check for surveillance. His pucker factor instantly intensified as he processed how fucked he was. His odds were slim to none if these guys knew what they were doing.

Then headlights stung his eyes before he noticed an illuminated taxi sign. Scott waved and lunged for the passenger door as it stopped. He got in and said the first place that came to his mind. He felt his blood pressure go down as the taxi shifted into drive and rushed him over to a convenience store a few blocks from his home. He checked his surroundings, paid the driver, and started down a surveillance detection route, or SDR, to get the drop on anyone waiting to ambush him. The SDR helped him sober up and he was pleasantly surprised to see no bad guys in position when he arrived. These people were amateurs, probably local goons.

But someone had sent them. It was long past time for Scott to go on the offensive.

He spent the following Saturday preparing his counterattack. First, to identify his enemy, he googled Nashville Police Lt. Wilson. The first result was an individual by the name of Josh Tyler Wilson. He then logged into one of the legal research services he and Mark used for tracking people. The name brought up multiple matches but only one was a police officer in and around Nashville. The fee required for the service subscription paid off when one needed it. A few more minutes of reading and clicking led Scott to a possible home address. Mapquest.com showed that, if he did indeed live there, he was within walking distance of several churches and multiple restaurants.

This gave Scott the impression that if Wilson took Sunday off, which someone of his rank most likely would, he would probably spend a good amount of the day on foot. This would give Scott an opportunity to follow him and gather intelligence on the opposition.

After lunch, Scott got to work on creating a covert device for listening and recording. He opened the boxes that contained his belongings to pull out two cheap, unused cellphones, an old MP3 player from his college days, and a retractable pen. He took them all apart and reassembled the pen and the digital audio player with components from the phones. This would have been impossible with the new smartphones that had debuted on the market a few years ago. The pen would function as a "bug" when the top was clicked; the digital player would enable Scott to listen via headphones and save the audio in an MP3 file.

Scott went to bed early and got up while it was still dark to get eyes on Wilson's apartment complex. He picked up breakfast and coffee from a fast-food chain, parked a couple blocks away, and walked to an alley he had spotted during his online research. It provided near-perfect concealment as the neighborhood awoke with the rising sun and Wilson emerged two hours later.

Indeed, the man walked to a nearby Baptist church. Scott followed from a distance but decided against going in. Wilson would definitely recognize him and a congregant would notice a visitor and draw attention by introducing himself. Instead, he spent an hour and a half sitting on a bench across the street before a crowd began bubbling out. He walked away when he saw Wilson flanked by a legion of walker-wielding retirees. Scott hung back until he saw Wilson walking on his own down a sidewalk. He tailed from a safe distance before Wilson stopped at a restaurant. Scott kept walking and glanced through the window as he passed. Wilson pulled a chair and sat at a table occupied by an elderly woman.

It was the same woman he had seen leading Hiram Parry at gunpoint through a haze of morning mist.

Hell yeah, Scott said to himself, they're losing the initiative to me. Their loss is my gain.

He turned a corner and walked to the back of the building where every restaurant had a dumpster and employees took their smoke breaks. Scott took out a lighter and offered it to a waiter who was having trouble lighting his cigarette. He started a conversation and learned the younger man's name was Andres. Scott suggested Spanish when Andres seemed to have difficulty with English; Andres appreciated it. Scott took out the pen, clicked it, and offered Andres fifty dollars to put it on a table next to the booth in the furthest-left corner. He gave Andres cash and put on the headphones. It didn't take long before he heard glasses and utensils clanking, and a dozen separate discussions.

Finally, he recognized Wilson talking to a female with a metallic Southern drawl. He regretted not getting the bug to them sooner, but if he had learned anything working for the Agency, it was that perfect was the enemy of the good.

A few minutes of ordering and pleasantries led to Wilson stating, "I told you I'd keep an eye out if anything related to our problematic friend came up. Something has."

"I thought they said it was an accident," the woman replied.

"My people did," Wilson replied. "But a P.I. showed up at my workplace earlier this week. He works for Mark Laurent."

"You told me that bastard wouldn't be a problem anymore."

"He hasn't been. But apparently he and this new guy saw you with Hiram."

"What? How?"

"They were walking in the woods when you were marching Hiram from the house to the barn."

"Oh, sheee-iiit. What do we do, now?"

"I called Blue Eyes."

"Old Blue Eyes? I thought he was retired."

"He'll make an exception in return for a large payday. We need a professional to deal with those P.I.s. I can cover half the fee but this problem is yours just as much as it is mine."

"Fine, I'll cover the other half. You know I'm good for it."

Well, that sounds ominous as hell, Scott thought. His recently-gained confidence dimmed just a little. The meal went on and Wilson paid the bill before they left. Scott had everything he needed but also did not want to leave evidence behind. So he paid Andres an additional fifty to retrieve the pen. Part of him disliked running people as assets, like he did Andres; it was manipulative. But his survival now appeared to depend on it. He knew he would not be able to take on Josh Wilson and the woman by himself. He needed Mark. If that meant he had to turn Mark, then so be it.

Scott went to the office after dark and called his boss from the landline. A vague question-and-answer session prompted Mark to say he would arrive shortly. His tone gave Scott the impression he was bringing his KA-BAR; he may have been projecting, given the fact he was conceal-carrying both of his pistols at that moment. Mark arrived shortly after 9:00 PM and entered the building without turning any lights on. Scott was sitting at his desk, illuminated by outside light pollution.

"What the fuck is this about?" Mark asked.

"Are you friends with a Lieutenant Josh Wilson?" Scott asked.

He made what looked like a grimace in the dim light. "I've met him. Why?"

"That young man we saw being held at gunpoint was found dead. Your friend may've killed the poor guy, himself."

"How long have—"

"Does the name Old Blue Eyes mean anything to you? Wilson mentioned him."

Mark's face suddenly looked like his blood had run cold. "When?"

"Our bad lieutenant and that woman you said you knew got together for brunch this morning. Or,

Sunday dinner, as my folks would call it. I managed to get a snippet of their dialogue on this."

Scott held up the MP3 player, took out the headphones, and played a minute of their conversation through the speakers. Mark's eyes widened as he grasped the danger they were both in and that Scott had discovered what he had tried to keep secret.

"Who is Old Blue Eyes, Mark? How do you know him, and Wilson, and the woman…what's her name?"

"Bonnie Johnson. Look, I've only heard stories about him. He's the guy you call when someone is about to turn state's evidence against you. When you need a witness silenced and that witness happens to be someone who's killed for you, you need someone who's very good at killing to kill the killer. Old Blue Eyes is the guy you call for hard targets in Tennessee, at least until very recently. People say he retired but I never believed that."

"So he works freelance? What about the others?"

"Wilson and Johnson are distant relatives; that's how these things are usually set up. They're affiliated, or at least acquainted, with the Dixie Mafia."

"Okay, um…you can't be serious. Is that what they actually call themselves?"

Mark's nostrils flared. "Laugh if you want, motherfucker. They traffic more dope, cook more crank, pay more bribes, pimp more kids, sell more guns, fence more stolen goods, and bury more bodies than *any* other organized crime outfit in the South. Go ahead. Laugh at their fucking name."

It took Scott a moment to process the verbal dossier that had just been thrown at him. "Goddamn. How do you figure into all this?"

Mark took a deep breath. "You work this job long enough, especially when you're trying to pay bills and you take the wrong kind of clients because you need the money, you'll run into some really bad people. Somebody sued Bonnie Johnson five years ago and their lawyers hired me to investigate the incident. Lieutenant Wilson showed up at my door one morning saying that he found drugs in my car. He was the only cop there and he said he was letting me off with a warning. If I didn't drop the Johnson case, his colleagues would find more in my house. A week later, the person who sued Bonnie died in a car accident. That's what Wilson's people called it."

Scott silently wondered how the hell he had ended up in a mess like this. "I applied for this job because I wanted to learn from the best. You were the best teacher I could've found for the stuff we do every workday. But this? Let's keep it real. I have slightly more experience with this stuff. I'm not saying it was an everyday occurrence, but we are taught how to break up networks. You and I need to dismantle this one. ASAP."

"Just how do we go about doing that?"

"Does that mean you're in?" Scott responded.

"You think I like looking over my shoulder for these people every day? I've wanted to get rid of them for years. But, how do we do that?"

"Divide and conquer. Pit them against each other. Johnson has the money and Wilson has the firepower. We could convince her that he's going to double-cross her and take the cash."

"That would be in character, knowing him."

"So, in the interest of full disclosure, I should say that I have two concealed firearms on my person, at this moment. Is it a problem if I slowly reach for one by the barrel and loan it to you? For your protection. I've never seen you carry and I wasn't sure if you keep any at home."

"Slowly," Mark replied.

Scott gently pulled the Berretta M9 from a holster on his ankle and handed it to Mark. "We need to take no chances from here on out. We've both got targets on our backs."

Mark accepted the pistol and Scott felt a returning small remnant of the trust they had recently lost. The next morning, they went to a nearby gun range to familiarize themselves with their weapons. Time on the range helped clear their minds and prepare them for the risks ahead. After a small lunch, they got in Mark's SUV and drove out to Bonnie Johnson's farmhouse. They parked near a barn made of rotting wood and walked to her front door with their weapons drawn.

Mark rang the doorbell and Bonnie called out, "Coming!"

She cracked open the door but stopped when she saw who it was.

"Good morning, Ms. Johnson. I was wondering if you could answer some ques–"

He stopped when he saw a long piece of wood and metal moving to his face. He grabbed the shotgun with both hands, pulled it out of Bonnie's hands, and stepped back while Scott kicked the door in, aimed the Smith & Wesson Model 625 at her and screamed for her to put her hands on her head. She stepped back with the same look in her eyes one usually saw in a fawn on a road. Mark closed the door and kept an eye on Bonnie while

Scott cleared the house. He shouted, "Clear!" at each room then returned to the front entrance.

"We know about Old Blue Eyes, ma'am," Scott said. "Did the price you were given sound normal to you?"

"He's retired. I figured it wouldn't be cheap."

"Wilson has the muscle, you have the money," Mark added. "Notice anything there, ma'am?"

The fear in her face dimmed into suspicion. "What are you saying?"

"Have either of y'all ever gotten rid of a relative?" Scott asked. "Is that a line y'all would never cross?"

Bonnie was silent for a few moments. "You're saying…I'm on the list."

"I don't know. Are you? Would Josh Wilson do that? You know him a lot better than we do."

Her breathing became faster and her eyes widened. Scott could tell that experiences from long ago were invading her thought process.

"When is he coming to collect your half of Old Blue Eyes' money?" Mark asked.

"In a few minutes," she replied. "I thought he was here early when y'all knocked."

Scott and Mark looked at each other; both managed to avoid saying *oh shit*. That was the exact moment they heard a car pull up the driveway.

"Upstairs," Bonnie commanded. "Now. I'll get him out of here as fast as I can."

Both did as they were told, despite their reservations. Their guts told them that she had as much incentive as they did to help get Wilson. And they had overestimated how much time they had left to prevent the hit from being arranged.

Scott and Mark hid in a small guest bedroom until they heard four gunshots from downstairs. They immediately bounded down the stairs and through the hall with their pistols in a two-handed grip. They cleared the kitchen before they spotted Bonnie standing over a man lying on his stomach in the living room.

Lieutenant Josh Wilson had four red holes in his back. Vapor drifted off the SCCY CPX pistol in Bonnie's hands. She stood next to a painting which suited the moment — a young woman with flowers in her hair, jewels in her clothing, and gargoyle wings sprouting out of her back. Scott and Mark aimed at her but failed to hide their astonishment.

Bonnie slid her gun back into a purse. "Josh has friends in the police department. People who will take matters into their own hands if the courts don't give them what they want. Our safest option is to hide all the evidence. Including this body. Are y'all gonna help me out or what?"

Scott and Mark glanced at each other. Mark shrugged and Scott said, "This is fucked up."

They rolled Josh Wilson in a carpet and covered it with plastic before they put him in the trunk of Bonnie's sedan. They drove down a forested trail in Bonnie's backyard to a place out of sight or earshot from civilization. Scott got the impression this was not the first time Bonnie had done this. Their journey was silent until Bonnie piped up.

"Y'all like brisket?"

Neither man answered, distracted by the road and the corpse they were about to hide, along with their reasons why.

"There's a place just outside the nearest town. Best barbeque in the state of Tennessee," she said. "Tender pork sandwiches on toasted buns, baked beans like you wouldn't believe. Puts anything in Memphis to shame."

Scott said nothing but found himself remembering talking to an insurgent leader during his third deployment to Iraq. It was after he had switched from Infantry to the Military Intelligence MOS. *Talked to* was sugarcoating it; he was part of a team interrogating the detainee with the help of a translator. The captured terrorist was accused of heinous crimes — murder, torture, dismembering dead bodies and live victims for fun. He glibly admitted to every one of them. He would go on and on describing what it looked, felt, and smelled like to cut a man's throat back and forth with a small knife until the vertebrae finally separated from the skull. Then, he would seamlessly switch to talking nostalgically about his favorite movie or reminiscing about the art classes he took before the Crusaders invaded his country.

It was clear to Scott that Bonnie Johnson was someone like that. A person who could commit a premeditated murder and, in the next breath, start talking about her book club as though nothing had just happened. No wonder she was the one who took care of Hiram Parry. Hell, she probably enjoyed doing it.

"What in the hell was all this about?" Scott muttered.

"Hmm?" Bonnie replied. Mark gave him a quick look, then returned his focus to the road.

"I'm just tryin' to figure out how you got involved in the mess that we later got dragged into. Really, what was this all about? What did that young man, Hiram, do?"

"Oh," Bonnie reclined in her seat. "Well...he was unreliable."

"What does that mean?" Scott turned his head to look at her. The car bumped up and down but he kept his focus on her.

"Hiram would show up late, probably because he was getting high on what he was supposed to sell for us. We supplied. He distributed to customers. Those were the rules. Lately, he'd show up with the money he was supposed to bring us...but a single-digit percentage would be missing. I talked to him about it once, twice, more than that...he'd always say that the customer had shortchanged him and it wouldn't happen again. But it did. Eventually, Josh and I decided we couldn't trust him."

The car bumped up and down again.

"Y'all murdered a young man because he was incompetent at his job?" Scott asked.

Bonnie stared back at him and he half-expected her to pull out her pistol, remembering what happened to the dead man currently in the trunk.

"I've been involved in this longer than you've been alive," she said. "Maybe twice as long. I've been breaking the law every day since before I had my first period and never once been arrested, not once. You know why? Because I'm organized and careful. I haven't lasted this long because I tolerate obvious time bombs like Hiram. With someone like him, an undisciplined fuck-up going from one last chance after another, it's not a matter of *if* he gets arrested and spills everything, but *when*. I protect myself by making them disappear."

Scott snorted and shifted back into a normal sitting position. He focused on the forest and was surprised when Bonnie spoke up again.

"Honestly, I didn't even see y'all when I was walking Hiram down to the shed. I was focused on him, everything in front of us, keeping the gun pointed proper like, in case he tried anything; it was just…tunnel vision, you know?"

Neither man replied.

They parked in a clearing, technically still on Bonnie's property, close to where they first saw her leading Hiram Parry to his doom. They got out and started digging with two shovels provided by their host. Bonnie leaned on the hood of her sedan. They were sweaty and swearing. Mark was the first to need a break and took a moment to get a Nalgene water bottle from the car. Scott kept digging while Bonnie Johnson quietly reached for the pistol in her purse and aimed at his back.

Seven shots rang out.

Scott turned to see Bonnie on the ground and Mark standing with his M9 in a weaver stance. They stared at each other.

Mark said, "She was going to—"

"Yeah, she almost did," Scott interrupted.

Mark nodded and asked, "We cool now?"

Scott nodded back. "Yeah. Thanks, bro."

"We need to wrap her up and keep digging. This hole ain't yet big enough for them both."

Mark used his experience investigating homicides for NCIS to instruct Scott on scrubbing the evidence from Bonnie's house and vehicle. Even still, they agreed the safest option for both of them was to leave town. Scott's six-month apprenticeship was almost over. He could take the State's exam in Memphis and then leave Tennessee for good. Florida, Georgia, Louisiana, and North Carolina all had reciprocity agreements for state-level licenses.

They spent the next two weeks finishing the cases they had left and preparing to move away. On their last night in Nashville, they went out to the bar they had gone to after their first day working together.

"I'm going to Michigan," Mark said. "They've got a lot of insurance cases up there. I'll find a space to rent and get started in a few months. What about you?"

A Blue Moon beer in a tall glass and Macallan Scotch, neat, arrived as Scott answered. "I'm going to travel for a while, visit some places I've wanted to return to. I'm not sure where I'll settle, probably Georgia or Texas."

"Wherever you end up, you'll do well. You're not bad at this."

Scott nodded. "I had a good teacher."

"And you don't give up when most people do. That's a gift and a curse. Did I ever tell you about the time I was in BUD/S training?"

"No. I had no idea you did that."

"I saw a vast majority of the people around me quit. I didn't but…I ended up breaking my leg when a stress fracture turned into a full break over time. I was given the option to recycle once I was healed or try out for something else. That's why I ended up in SWCC instead of the SEAL teams. Every individual has a different limit, but everybody has one. I got in over my head with Josh and Bonnie. I tried to handle it on my own. That was a mistake."

"Well, whether we like how it turned out or not, it's fixed now."

Scott packed his red pickup truck the next morning and moved out of the room he had lived in for months. He drove to a BBQ restaurant in the Bellevue neighborhood, near I-40. He had one last lunch planned with Brianna before leaving for good. Over pork and chicken covered in spicy sauce, with fries and beans on the side, they had a friendly conversation about future plans and bands from the Sixties. The meal would not have been complete without large cups of Coca-Cola, the nectar of the American Southeast.

"I'll be right back," Scott said when he needed the restroom.

"Cool," Brianna replied.

He got up and was surprised when another man bumped into him.

"Oh, I'm sorry," an old voice said with an Appalachian mumble. "I wasn't paying attention."

Scott told him, "It's fine, sir."

Then Scott got a good look at him. Over the age of seventy. Crooked back. A hairless head covered with a dozen lines visible on the skin. And two wide, blue eyes covered by thick-rim glasses.

The old man nodded and shuffled away to a table. He was the only other occupant. Scott had not noticed him despite the fact he was trained to notice everyone who came in or left the room. This guy knew how not to stand out. To someone with Scott's background, that made the old man stand out even more.

Scott used the bathroom with extreme caution and thanked the good Lord that nobody followed him in there. He paid for his and Brianna's food before they said their goodbyes in the parking lot. Scott wished her luck on her music career before getting in his pickup. He stuffed the Smith & Wesson Model 625 into his pants before he drove out and merged onto the highway. He regretted not buying a proper holster.

A few minutes went by before something in Scott's subconscious, most likely a remnant of his training at The Farm, compelled him to engage in an SDR. He got off at the first exit and turned toward a Starbucks on the right. He engaged his turn signal and noticed a beige sedan behind him. He turned off the signal and kept going straight until a fork in the road prompted a left turn. The sedan made the same turn and Scott stayed within the speed limit as structures were gradually replaced by trees and bushes. Whoever was following him only had one vehicle, as long as nothing was following him in the air.

He felt alert but also relaxed as training and experience crept in from his memory. He knew how to think on his feet, how to lure an adversary to disadvantageous ground. There was no perfect option, but perfect was the enemy of good, of possible. Once they were surrounded by vast plots of farmland with no other people in sight, Scott pulled over to the side of the road and stopped. He shifted the pistol to the small of his back. The M9 was long gone, disassembled and thrown into a river. Another thing he regretted, now.

Scott got out of his truck as the sedan pulled over and stopped. He had a feeling in his stomach that reminded of guarding checkpoints in Iraq, where acting too slowly could get him or other Marines killed but moving too quickly could result in innocent people dying. He kept his hand close to his concealed pistol as the old man from the restaurant slowly stepped out of his car.

"Can I help you, sir?" Scott asked.

Old Blue Eyes gave a friendly smile but something about him, maybe an aura, appeared to not be alive. The last time Scott had seen someone like that was Kasem al-Mana, a Qatari intelligence officer who defected to al-Qaeda. He had never forgotten the look of a man who was familiar with death and appeared unafraid of it. Someone who carried himself like a phantom and vanished in large crowds.

"Well, I was wondering if you could help me," the old man said. "I'm looking for a couple friends of mine. They haven't returned my calls for a couple of weeks."

To keep himself calm, Scott thought it'd be fucking hilarious if this retiree dropped him after everything he's survived. But that old man potentially spent hours practicing everyday; he could still have lightning-quick reflexes. He realized the old man came after him because he was the first one to skip town; Mark would be next, after this.

"Josh Wilson and Bonnie Johnson," Old Blue Eyes mumbled. "You know those folks. That's not a question."

Adrenaline flooding Scott's system drowned out the old man's quiet delivery.

Three gunshots rang out in the Tennessee countryside.

Dark clouds started to drop rain.

Sean Liam Hastings is an up-and-coming writer of short and long-form fiction from Sandy Springs, Georgia.

His overactive imagination, along with a lifelong obsession with spies and detectives, has led him to craft a fictional universe based on the dark and dangerous aspects of our real world. He graduated from Oglethorpe University in 2018 with a Bachelor's in History and a minor in Writing.

He is creator/host of podcast "Get Real on Iran", available on Soundcloud.

His character Scott Larson will be featured in Hastings' forthcoming novel.

facebook.com/seanliamhastings
Twitter: @4_hastings

Skatin' on Thin Ice in a Self-Cleanin' Oven

CK Stephens

Southie, 1970

Rounding the corner to the Haunty's open basement door, Sean sees Johnny B tied tight to a heavy wooden chair. Instinctively ducking outta sight, he struggles to quiet the traitorous rasping of his breath. Slipping into hiding, his body freezes in fear of discovery. Ears on overdrive, Sean instantly plans escape routes from all directions.

Sean's view of the basement is only the lower half of chairs and legs, two tied, four standing, two walking. Rope restraints at the man's wrists irritate already raw, bloodied skin where he once struggled, but no longer. Sean smells terror rising up the stairway through the open door.

He hears one of Whitey's lieutenants roughly remind Johnny of how things work in South Boston when The Man gives orders. Then talk is over. Sean catches a low flash of silver as a knife slashes.

This is Sean's wake-up call.

Will he hear it in time?

* * * * *

Southie, 1965

Part boy, part man, Sean daily skated on thin ice between Good and Evil in this Southie world where the FBI eagle-eyes the Guineas instead of the Micks. Where Micks turned Guineas into favored FBI scapegoats so drugs and prostitution and business payoffs become their doings. Where cops called Southie a self-cleaning oven, a term given while they sat back in the early sixties as Irish Mob gangsters rubbed each other out. God, but it had been bloody. Bodies in the street every day or getting disappeared without a trace.

Then Whitey got out of Alcatraz. All that killing cleared the way for him. Made it easy to move into power to lead the Irish Mob. The timing of the man's return to his old stomping grounds sure couldn't have been planned better than that. To this day, Whitey's still Master of the Hustle. Always playing the stupid Feds against the Italian Mob. Has the audacity to run his crime ring right under their noses.

The Man is nearly mythical. Triple O's Lounge is his headquarters. Like a leering spider, he manipulates from the center of a complex web, offering his henchmen either doggish loyalty or three burial options: the too-early but more respectable traditional pine box; the sudden slippery muck at river's edge; or a danger-infested prison cell where a price on their heads means they won't last long.

This is the world Sean lived in. This is the world he sought to make his mark in.

This is the world where a starry-eyed, impractical young boy plays at being a bad man and gets his first real glimpse of personal danger with casually quick-drawn blood, with fear and terror. A world where he grows up.

A world where he must make a decision.

Sean had been initiated into the Irish Mob back in fifth grade. He was called The Little Prince because he slipped through tough spots without a scratch.

"Such a charming boy!" Sean mimics the project's trusting old ladies, then throws his head back, laughing sarcastically. He flicks the butt of a filched cigarette to let it sizzle in the damp, leaf-clogged gutter of the project's neglected street.

Fearless founder and leader of his own small gang of boys, Sean carries himself well as a pass-down from his father's military service. Thanks to street smarts gleaned while surviving eight years in Southie, the teen is comfortable as leader. Though a bit short, Sean has the automatic edge on leadership as he seems tallest of his gang. He can almost look Lil' Donnie, his best friend, in the eye, but only because the bulky six-footer slouches as if to disguise his height. Hard Irish to his bones, Sean is endowed with an uncanny ability to detect trouble. His boys never take a pinch, so they long ago changed his nickname to Street Prince.

Sean keeps them on the outer edges of trouble, so far with a stellar record of safety. Steering his lads well away from Whitey's Triple O's Lounge across from the Broadway T stop, Sean is always careful that they only do small stuff so no one gets hurt. Sure, they bruise a knee or skin an elbow from scrambling over fences, but nothing serious.

Pickpocketing in crowds is a rush, but Sean taught them to never snatch a lady's purse. Raise too much stink and they could get caught with evidence. The challenge is all about staying under the cop radar. Raids in better parts of town usually get them some bucks or cool stuff to hock.

A few years back, Sean and Lil' Donnie got bored with their tame stuff and small takes. Looking for thrills, Sean learned of the Mulroney Gang. Their young men were a bit older and involved in heavier stuff. They'd heard of Sean and appreciated his skills — fast fingers and a quick, analytic, problem-solving mind.

So Sean and Lil' Donnie sometimes cross the river to where the tainted smell of diesel slick rises from badly polluted saltwater to mix with brisk ocean breezes carrying an overlay of offal from the catch of the day. Where seagulls, white feathers glinting sunlight against a deep blue sky, trail inbound fishing boats and wheel overhead, shrieking and fighting for position amidst each violent plunge to the sterns.

Today, Sean and Lil' Donnie slouch against clammy concrete, pretending to lounge in their well-positioned corner of the docks while waiting to meet their Mob contact here on the other side.

Sean is ever reminded to stay way below the signs of Whitey, that psycho gangster who smiles at you one minute and kills you the next. So the two boys work with the Mulroney gang only occasionally, and always on the far outer fringes of Whitey's active Killeen-Winter Hill gang.

They aren't stupid.

* * * * *

Southie, 1970

At the Haunty, Sean immediately looked around stealthily to make sure no one was near before he ducked outta sight but where he could still watch. Now he sees Whitey's top lieutenant whip a switchblade out of his boot and hears the fearsome sound of its opening click.

The man growls, "Boy, you messed up bad. Talkin' too much with them Guineas. You know those two are off-limits. Better tell me. What you were rattin' to 'em?"

"I weren't tellin' 'em nothing. They was just friends of me girlfriend."

"Mebbe we should have a little talk with the Guinea girl? Bettah yet, mebbe yer wife? Little wifey know about that sweet piece?"

Johnny cried. "No, no. Please, I won't ever see that girl or her friends again. I promise."

Sean watched legs bend as the goon screamed, "And just how will we know that?"

"I give you my word on the Bible. I'll never speak with her again," screeched Johnny B.

"Hah! Ya mean ya won't ever lay her again, right? Lemme give you my word as a sign." The goon struck fast, slicing Johnny B in the groin. He snarled, "Just a reminder — next time ya mess up, I'm not gonna miss yer artery."

Through Johnny B's banshee scream, the goon wiped the dripping crimson knife on the pants leg of a howling Johnny B. "Ah, shut yer trap. It's just a scratch compared to what we could do to ya. But, ya make another mistake, we'll give ya a real nice funeral — if we're feelin' generous."

The other goons laughed but sounded jumpy like they knew it could be their turn next time.

"Or mebbe we'll just disappear ya."

Nervous goons laughed raucously, loud enough to cover Johnny's howls of pain.

Sweet Jesus. Seeing Johnny B get cut, Sean's smart enough to understand this is his personal wake-up call. Knowing Whitey's frequent use of the Mob's limited burial options, Sean decides to live, which means he'll have to take on the risk of finding a good escape route.

Before the goons finish laughing, Sean slips out without a sound. Looks over his shoulder for weeks, but finally figures they hadn't seen him. Knows this in his gut because he is still on this side of the ground. It forces him to face the danger. Always thought he was such a hotshot; but he was just a dumb kid. Getting out of Whitey and the Mob's clutches becomes a full-time job. But how to do it and still help Ma?

Sean's da is dead so they need the income. Ma suspects but never really has any proof of her son's shenanigans. Surviving the best he can in this hopeless place, Sean lives in the shadows, making sure the cops never have reason to knock heavily on their door in the middle of the night.

Sean's ma had better never find out how deep he'd been in. Might not want to let him escape to anywhere, but he bet she knew he had to get away. He had to figure out how to leave or he'd get trapped in the Mob and likely face death at Whitey's hands.

For some reason, Sean keenly sensed that coming out of this situation alive and well would benefit him in a very different, but unknown future. But for the life of him, he didn't know why he felt that so strongly about that future — and certainly couldn't even imagine how or where his life could improve.

* * * * *

Southie, 1975

After miserable years of sidestepping Whitey's control, Sean was a junior in high school and his earlier escape hunch finally paid off. Thanks to his school advisor's forceful urging, Sean agreed to apply to a few colleges. To his surprise, he received an offer of a full scholarship to attend the University of California at Santa Cruz.

Sean suddenly saw college out of state as his only escape from the unavoidable end of the evil life Whitey offered hidden behind the addictive lure of money and power. Sean accepted the scholarship but had not the slightest idea that his move to California would be only the first step on his way to a drastically altered existence he'd tried to imagine but couldn't even conjure up.

Choosing to live life without fear meant leaving his family behind. A huge price to pay, for sure, but he was worth more to them alive than six feet under. Ma drove him crazy with worry. Though he had deep misgivings about leaving her and his younger brother behind in possible danger, he simply knew he had to go.

Anybody who tried to leave Whitey's gang was always seen as a risk. So, Sean had done it slow. Did it smart. He watched out for his own backside and kept his Ma and little brother safe. It was all about maneuvering and playing gang politics.

Still, the promise of Mob-threat hung over Sean. Whitey's goons repeatedly fell in next to him, sauntering alongside, tossing out strong suggestions that it would be in his best interest to return to their lucrative and protective brotherhood of working for The Man — or else.

Then they'd sweeten the pot a bit. "Look, jus' a little help here 'n there. Good money, eh boy?"

"Yeah, I know. I know," Sean answered. "But I can help Whitey more by going to college."

"Oh sure, boy. That's a good ' un. Tell me anothah," a goon mocked.

Sean stopped cold and turned on the man, going for broke, risking everything in hopes word would get back to The Man. Menacingly, Sean said, "Look, you don't seem to get it. I pick up a degree in accounting, I come back and help hide Whitey's assets but still have them liquid at the same time. It's all about takin' care of the family. You dig?"

Leaving day arrived and a few days later Sean found himself alone on a most unusual college campus. Before he had time to process his arrival, he began to meet people; his strong accent made him stand out. A couple of students helped him sign up for classes. Trusting strangers was new to him, but once in classes he made good friends with a select few.

Fascinated by medieval history, Sean took a class which led to additional study with a group of guys, then building and testing their authentic weapons of the period. They enjoyed it so much that, after six months of practice, the group put on a Medieval Festival. Re-enactors came all the way from San Jose to participate.

By the end of his first year, Sean and his two closest friends, Ian and Sheila, had saved up enough to go to Ireland for a glorious two weeks.

The night before they were to fly back to the States, Ian bet him twenty five dollars he couldn't stay alone overnight in the ruins of the burial cairn they had just visited. Sean took the bet. After all, he'd been in worse places. Easy money.

Ireland, 1440

Sean woke up, but he couldn't find his friends. The burial cairn was not in ruins but looked repaired. There were no planes in the sky. There were no cars. He saw a figure in the distance dressed in clothes the likes of which they wore in the re-enactments.

He laughed and thought maybe he was more scared than he had let on the night before. After all, if he thought the cairn was in ruins, he had to have been scared because here it was in great shape. But the figure in the distance was all alone and there were no tents hawking souvenirs or loudspeakers blaring when the next tour would take place.

Sean would soon find this new old world was full of intrigue, danger, and pivotal choices that echoed the drama and dangers of his younger years. He'd quickly learn his time in Southie had been but partial preparation for this far tougher and vastly crueler world of medieval Ireland.

Strangely enough, Sean recognized eerie similarities between the Ireland of the 1440s and the South Boston of 1970s. There was one shared rule across the ages that Sean understood and for which he had arrived fully prepared:

I want what you have and will take it unless you can stop me.

But which side would he land on in this time? What would the past bring to his future?

CK Stephens has always been a traveler. However, once she experienced Western Ireland's Bunratty Castle, she had to write about it. The short story submitted for this anthology is based on Sean, the main character of the soon-to-be-published *An Irish Prince: A Future Past*. The novel shifts to fifteenth century Ireland, a very different place, yet with eerie similarities to the Southie described here about Sean's life in South Boston's projects of 1970.

scfk2019@gmail.com

Judgie

Jason B. Sheffield

One of the perks of being a police officer is playing crazy 911 calls at the annual Christmas party. In such company, even a murder call can be eggnog-through-the-nostrils hilarious. One favorite of the City of Atlanta police force was that of the perp "Danny".

Following Vietnam, Danny had spent less than a year in the psych ward before he escaped in a doctor's coat and no pants. Sprayed with just about every known plant killer the US government could manufacture during the Vietnam War, Danny swallowed more than his share. That, combined with the usual tragedies of war, made him one seriously charred cookie crumb sunk into the deep recesses of the VA's conventional oven.

When the 911-dispatch operator got a somewhat unintelligible call from a Japanese pawnshop owner named Abraham Chen, she snapped her fingers at a co-worker and pointed at her headset. This was going to take the cake.

Chen whispered hysterically into the butt of the phone, as he ducked behind his Formica countertop. Danny whistled curt positional calls and signaled for his platoon to forge ahead to the mouth of the river; "Charlie" was close by. The operator nearly busted out when Chen said, "I no Charlie! I Abraham!"

Eleven years later in 1986, Danny would get out again, this time on purpose. With the number of patients rising exponentially and Reagan's plan to opt out of domestic social reform and focus on international capitalism, Veterans Memorial didn't have funding or enough bed space to care. They opened the cage and turned Danny loose on society. Danny, however, wasn't ready and neither was society.

Danny didn't have much family, and he assumed the family he had was sure to reject him. The last he heard, his mother had moved two thousand miles away, and his older brother was a gambler who, as a man about town, would never want Danny as a wingman. As for his father, Danny felt like he didn't want him before and that he certainly wouldn't now. He'd be alone again.

His nightmares and tremors returned.

The summer before Danny's release, I had turned eleven. It was 1985 and I was enjoying French kissing and hand-over-the-sweater kind of stuff. More importantly, my nosy, single mother, Carter Scales, was busy with her career as a criminal defense attorney, as she had reached a professional and personal zenith of her own that kept her out of my business.

Professionally speaking, she was in total control of her career. She knew the bumps and dips of working criminal defense cases in the City of Atlanta. At times, it was a lot like working the urinals at a movie theater; it had its adventures. But she finally had the respect of prosecutors, judges and juries. A woman not on the rise but arrived.

It was then she met a true prince, although he was parading around as a good ol' boy judge.

Denver sat as a senior judge on the criminal and civil trial calendar in the City of Atlanta Municipal Court and adored Mom's belligerent ways. He was a country boy who had come up. The son of an auctioneer, Denver spoke surprisingly slowly and without much flair. He was an artful speaker, though, who crafted his thoughts.

Their first semi-personal encounter occurred after she had lost a trial in his court. Denver called her back to his chambers to congratulate her on a well handled and diligently prepared trial despite the fact that she had lost. Denver was impressed and wanted to shake her hand. I happened to be present during their first meeting, as my babysitter had dropped me off at the courthouse. When Mom sat down in the more casual environment of his chambers, she watched him light up a cigarette and found herself barely able to breathe — and it wasn't the smoke.

"Tricky son of a gun, huh?" Denver said, minding his language due to the young boy in the room.

My mother never had heard a judge talk badly about a district attorney before. "Who? The D.A.?"

Denver nodded politely. "Don't care for him much. He's a real shark, but you handled yourself nicely."

"Thank you."

"It was a loser anyway."

"Well," she said with a smile, "if the jury had been able to hear Catherine's testimony, I don't think there's any way in hell they would have convicted."

"Colonel, the trial's over."

"Colonel" was a title many of the old judges called attorneys back in those days to place a name on their fighting spirit.

My mother sat there annoyed.

Denver laughed. "You are somethin' else." Clearly he'd never seen a woman with that much spark.

My mother had coarse, ropey, chestnut-colored hair and crystal blue eyes. She gave him a penetrating stare, and he offered her a cigarette. She held it as he extended his lighter, and she exhaled deeply. As she took another drag, she caught Denver watching her.

Mom rolled the edge of her cigarette in an amber ashtray and cocked her head. They held each other in an age-old stare. Neither ever recovered.

She kept her crushed cigarette as a memento of the smoke that changed her life. She loved to collect little symbolic things.

Denver was twenty two years older than my mother, who was now in her mid-thirties. He had soft facial features and the kindest Bassett Hound brown eyes. Under his robe, Denver was a cowboy. He collected pocketknives and guns and wore giant belt buckles, cowboy boots, and Levi's plaids with pearl snap buttons encased in silver.

She was young and feisty. Denver was a warm summer rain that washed a calm over her high-strung spirit. Although they argued, Denver's status as a judge continually kept Mom in check. Her career was her life, and she respected all aspects of it. Denver was both smart and witty, and she respected his knowledge and life experience. Denver knew exactly how to handle Mom's irrational temper and misguided insecurities. When my mother got madder than hell, he'd simply laugh at her, which of course pissed her off even more. It also convinced her that Denver was the man of her dreams. He took her just as she was. He never tried to push her like my father did. He never tried to change her like her father did.

Denver was also a kinder, gentler entrance into the bigoted Atlanta boys' club of the late '70s and early '80s. On Denver's arm, Mom got smiles and handshakes instead of double talk and sexual harassment. She went to barbecues, lake parties, wore cutoff jeans, and cowboy boots and hats. They skinny-dipped and drank moonshine and howled at the moon and laughed at the sunrise. He even made our being Jewish more acceptable to others.

Normally, when Southerners heard that we were Jewish, they'd twinge: "Jewish, huh? Didn't ch'all kill Jesus?"

Mom would just stare blankly and say, "Yes, that was my parents who did that."

With Denver by her side, though, people said, "Oh, how interesting," or "neat," as if being Jewish were some new type of vacuum cleaner that also polished silver.

I got my first real taste of Denver a few months later. My mother dressed me for a day of outdoor rumble and tumble — a day in the country — in an outfit she had purchased at Saks Fifth Avenue for $500: a pair of corduroy overalls, a cashmere cap and sweater, suede boots, and a pair of leather gloves.

She tried to explain Denver to me. How he was a very accomplished attorney like Momma was, how he could whittle any issue down to a grain of sand and then erect a skyscraper of an argument on its foundation. How he was a judge and respected by everyone he knew. I honestly didn't know what in the hell she was talking about.

As we drove into the country and the city dissolved behind us, Mom looked at me with Disney World eyes. By the time we arrived at his red-brick ranch, she was giddy.

"Isn't it great?" she marveled. All I saw was a front yard of dirt.

"You see those trees over there?" she asked, referring to lengthy row of green and red trees. "Those are apple trees. We're gonna make apple jelly."

I scoffed. "Strawberry's my favorite," I said, refusing to acknowledge any potential for fun.

As we stepped out of the car, I heard a rather unusual noise — a moan. I pulled my cap up over my ears and stood still until it repeated itself again. My mother faked a bewildered look.

"What could that be?" she asked.

I shrugged and ran to the back of the driveway and onto Denver's back porch that overlooked a quilt of fields stitched together with red and yellow trees.

Standing in the shade of a giant oak were a dozen of the fattest cows I'd ever seen. A baby named Mighty called out again, and my eleven-year-old intellect kicked into overdrive with an all-too-exciting realization.

"Cows, Momma. Cows!" I repeated the phrase, as if she were deaf or as if I had regressed in age six years. "I want one! Can I have one, please? Please, can I have one?"

"We're gonna have to ask Denver."

My mind was racing. You mean there's a chance I can have my own cow?! I thought.

By the time Denver came out, I was ready to shake his hand and accept him into our family. My mother put her tongue down his throat. I didn't care. She was helping my cause — putting in a good word with his tonsils, apparently.

Denver was a giant, but weathered and soft. A former University of Georgia nose guard, he was six-two and two hundred and thirty five pounds. Hugging him, though, was like embracing a giant pillow. I would later nickname him "Judgie".

That morning, I ran across the pasture toward the cows. The cool air pulled tears out of the corner of my eyes and my breath billowed like steam. I was thankful, indeed, for my cashmere hat and sweater, as well as my boots and leather gloves. I held little Mighty in my sights, as I sped across the pasture. With each leap, I could barely believe my luck. Life was immeasurable, perfect — that is, until my boots flew out from underneath me without warning and my head landed directly into the warmest patch of grass I'd ever experienced. Using my Saks Fifth Avenue leather gloves to pick feces and mucus out of my cashmere hat became one of my fonder memories of Judgie's farm. Judgie exploded with laughter.

Later that first day, I sat elevated fifteen feet off the ground in the mouth of a giant bulldozer and picked apples. At the top of the apple tree, there was nothing between the sky and me. Pure blue enveloped me, and I breathed absolute joy.

Upon entering Judgie's house for the first time, I dropped my armful of apples in exchange for what I thought was the better trade — a loaded twelve-gauge shotgun that leaned against the refrigerator. My mother freaked, in part, because after I picked it up, I spun around to show it to her with the barrel pointed at her torso.

"Look, Momma. A gun!"

She held her breath and walked calmly over to me, maintaining the all-too-fake smile of a weathered server. She gently removed the weapon of death from my hands.

"You were supposed to put these away," Mom told Judgie as she thrust the lengthy firearm into his chest.

"That's just what I'm going to do right now!"

"But Mom…" I said.

"No," she insisted.

Judgie loved his guns. There had to be at least two dozen handguns, shotguns, and rifles lying around as if the Wild West had sneezed its violent past over everything. Judgie frantically carried armfuls of weapons like firewood to the hall closet while my mom chewed him a new asshole. I felt bad for my new best friend.

Two months before Danny's release, my grandmother died. My mother drowned in sadness despite her fight to survive it. She felt like a little girl, robbed of her mommy. I told her I would take care of her; I would protect her and "be a man". I was twelve then. When she saw me crying while I was trying to console her, she called me a liar and scolded me.

"Some man you turned out to be!" she said.

Judgie tried to comfort me. "She doesn't know what she's saying. Your grandmother was very important to her."

Judgie embraced his role as peacemaker. He stood up for me and did his best to create harmony between us all. With Mom so depressed over Grandma's death, Judgie became my closest friend. I told him I loved him.

As the weeks crept by, my mother found solitude in her work. Judgie was a good influence on her and was able to focus her attention off her mother and onto work — a case of a less fortunate soul who needed extra attention. Danny, the skittish war vet, was that case.

Four days before Danny's release, Judgie came to our house to speak to my mother about Danny and his complicated mental situation. The hospital's decision to release him was wrong. Judgie wanted to help Danny stay on track once out and not jump off an overpass before he could find him a proper place for further treatment. Judgie pushed my mother to get involved.

"Reagan has totally screwed this kid with these anti-funding initiatives," Judgie told her. "He's got a hearing coming up, and I need you to make an entry and represent the kid."

"You seem to know all about him. Plus, you and Judge Cooper are good friends. You'll probably get further faster."

Judgie drew inward. "I'm not the best person to handle it," Judgie said vaguely.

"Why not?"

"I need you to do it." Judgie looked at my mother, uncomfortable.

"What's the matter with you?"

"He cannot be released, Carter. He's a danger to himself and society. He's a perfect case for commitment, and I..." Judgie searched for words. The combination of his demeanor and speechlessness confused my mother.

"Denver, who is this kid to you?" she asked him. He let out deep sigh. "*Denver,*" she insisted.

"He's my son."

Actually, Judgie had two sons: Danny, the schizophrenic, and Marty, the sociopath. He had never mentioned either. My mother put her hand to her chest to make sure her heart was still beating; it was ... and faster than usual.

Although Judgie loved his two boys dearly, he didn't have a relationship with either of them. Marty wanted Judgie's farmland and tried to use the threat of denying Judgie visits with his grandkids as leverage. Danny wanted a dark room and a soft pillow. Judgie couldn't manage either. And there was more bad news.

"Where is he going to stay?" my mother asked.

"With the ward being shut down, he'll be staying with … me."

"At your home?" she asked.

He grimaced. "It's only temporary," Judgie said.

My mother nearly fell over. "Living with *you*? What about Benjamin and me? How are we gonna have an *us*?"

Judgie clearly felt stuck. "He's my son. I can't abandon him like the hospital did."

My mother made up her mind. There were no options. Danny couldn't get out.

I had never seen my mother fight for something so hard. More focused on preserving her relationship with Judgie than truly helping Danny, she unloaded on the court system.

Danny was crazy. Period. He needed to be locked up or he would either kill himself or someone else. She didn't know whether it was true or not, but the exceptions to involuntary commitment necessitated that Danny be a danger to himself or others.

"He escaped before and practically called in reinforcements to destroy the Asian pawn shop owner," my mother told the judge.

"That may be, but in a shop full of guns, he didn't go after a single one," Judge Cooper said.

"They were locked up."

"If he were a true danger, don't you think he would have exercised his options on the owner of the shop? I don't have anything, Ms. Scales, to sink my teeth into."

"Well, maybe the police should have given him a few more minutes to see if he actually would have shot the guy and given us a dead body. Then maybe you could've *sunk your teeth into that!*"

Judge Cooper didn't appreciate her tone, but my mother knew she had the weight of Judgie behind her. She took extra liberties.

"Ms. Scales, these restrictions are tight. Believe me, I understand the position you're in — trust me — but my hands are tied. Even if I wanted to put him in, I've got nothing to base it on. I'm sorry."

She felt her relationship slipping away. "But, Your Honor, this is going to be devastating for everyone. He can't be released."

"You've done an excellent job, counselor. But I'm sorry. My ruling is that I deny your motion."

My mother's eyes fell with her heart.

"Release him," the judge said.

On the day of Danny's release, Judgie ate dinner at our house. As the candles burned down and the bottle of wine emptied out, the mood settled nicely for him to confess his sins of omission.

"I wasn't good to Danny or Marty…as a father."

"That's impossible," I interrupted. My mother grabbed my hand to shut me up.

"Thank you, son, but I was hard on my kids. I treated them like men, but they were only boys. Marty left to go be with his mother when he was fifteen, and I didn't fight it. Danny enlisted. Neither of 'em could stand me."

He was so humiliated about his failures. So open about it. I grabbed his hand then hugged his oversize neck. I'd never seen an adult apologize before.

After dinner and dishes, it had gotten late and I went up to bed. Mom asked Judgie to stay. He said he couldn't. He had to make sure Danny had gotten in okay.

"It's almost midnight," she told him.

"I know, darlin'. I'll be fine."

"It's forty five minutes from here."

I climbed out of bed and peeked down the stairwell. "Judgie?" I interrupted.

"Yes, son."

"If you stay here tonight, we can all sleep together. Like a slumber party."

He thought about it for a minute. "I tell you what — next weekend you got a deal."

I waved goodbye as Mom and Judgie headed out to the driveway. I went into my bathroom, which overlooked the driveway, and watched through the wooden blinds.

She made a few more pleas, and he politely said no. The cold air fell quietly between them, and there was nothing left to do but embrace goodbye.

As she stood next to his car, holding his hand and cuddling his neck, she noticed a nail on the driveway positioned behind his front tire. She told me about it years later. It was large and could have easily punctured it, had she not noticed. How the nail didn't flatten the tire on the way up was a mystery to her. He would surely not be so lucky on the way down.

Mom bent over and picked up the nail, clutching it in her hand. As she returned to his neck and hugged him and pressed her lips against the skin behind his ear, she had a very out-of-place thought — a random and meaningless thought. She imagined she could take that nail and stick it straight into his neck and pierce his carotid artery.

The thought of blood spurting out made her jerk her eyes shut. Judgie nudged her with his nose as if to wake her from a bad dream.

"Hey," he said. "You all right?"

"Yeah," she said, scoffing at herself. "Fine."

An hour and a half later, Judgie pulled into his driveway. The house lights were off. He entered the kitchen through the garage, turned them on and found a pan on the stove with eggs burnt to the bottom. A stick of butter sloped and softened on the countertop. Judgie smiled and returned the butter. He picked up the pan and soaked it in the sink. At least Danny was hungry. That had to be good.

Judgie looked around the kitchen. The place was a disaster. Mom had cleaned it every time we went up there, but he was just messy. Judgie and some of his buddies had gone hunting the week before, and the place was a wreck. Piles of newspapers and cashed cigars. Camouflage vests, duck whistles, rifles, and handguns. He wanted to straighten up the place before Danny came back, but the long task list led to procrastination and stagnation. So much to do. Too much to do. *Oh, well*, he probably thought, *I'll clean it up tomorrow.* With so many guns lying around, he failed to notice that one was missing.

Right around one a.m., give or take a ten minutes or so, Judgie decided to shave. He often found it difficult to sleep with an itchy beard. As he turned on the hot water in his first-story bathroom, the window overlooking his back porch steamed over, preventing him from seeing outside or the pair of eyes that watched him from three feet away. He gently pulled the razor down his left cheek. He didn't see the shadow. He rinsed the blade beneath the whistling tap. He didn't hear the whimpering. As he dragged the razor across his Adam's apple, he didn't see the gun tip touch the glass. The razor jerked and nicked his throat as the window crashed and a bullet exploded through the side of his neck, rupturing his carotid artery.

State Judge Murdered by Mentally Ill Son, the headlines read.

When Mom got the call from Judgie's neighbor, she collapsed in the kitchen and sobbed herself into a blithering heap at the base of the refrigerator. She bent into a slump and slept there until morning. Danny turned himself in three months later after living in the woods in the dead of winter.

Although no one was there to see Judgie's last moments, we were able to put them together. Danny must have seen Judgie as a Vietcong, or maybe he just wanted to kill his father after so many years of neglect. Either way, on the second go-round, there was no hesitation about Danny's involuntary commitment. Judge Cooper attended the funeral and cried like a little boy.

My mother hid her pain in anger again and shut herself down from feeling anything. She cursed herself for having opened up to someone, knowing that her luck wasn't that rich.

Marty instituted suit for Judgie's land. He wanted to flip the acreage into a neighborhood of single-family homes. My mother fought against him, trying everything she could to demonstrate that Marty was a looting bastard and that Judgie's intent was to leave the land to her and me. Marty, of course, won. Bulldozers came in the next day.

The apple trees became firewood.

I don't know what happened to the cows.

Every now and then, for the last thirty years, my mother would open her jewelry box and then one small drawer in particular. The drawer is lined with velvet and holds two objects: an old used-up cigarette and the nail she found that night. Sometimes she takes out the nail and clutches it in her hand; rolls it between her fingers; feels the weight of the metal, the sharpness of its tip.

She thinks back to the night of Judgie's death and their long goodbye — the goodbye she said while pressing her lips to his neck and her thought about sticking that nail in the exact spot where the bullet ultimately entered Judgie's neck.

She folds the nail in her fingers and returns it to the drawer and closes her eyes to her one inescapable thought: If only I hadn't noticed it.

Jason B. Sheffield is a practicing criminal defense trial attorney based out of Atlanta, Georgia. Jason was recently invited by the US Embassy in the Republic of Georgia (formerly part of the Soviet Union) to teach jury trial techniques to criminal defense attorneys after their constitution was amended to provide its citizens jury trials.

His first novel, *Son of a Bitch*, published in 2017, is a story about an attorney deciding whether or not to defend his mother at her disbarment hearing after she is caught *in flagrante delicto* with a client at the federal pen. Jason's passion for law, teaching and storytelling is second only to his love of his family.

Home

William Steven Farmer

Six-thirty in the morning and I was still trying to wake up. Big Bill Carson glanced over his tin coffee cup and grinned.

"Ready to save the world, Rook?"

I nodded, smiled, and began unloading my brown paper bag of eggs, bacon, and canned biscuits on the green Formica countertop. Chief Walker assigned me to Engine 5 C-shift, meaning I would be on Big Bill's engine. I couldn't believe my luck. Bill was a legend around the firehouse. He told the best war stories because he had run the best calls and survived. All the big fires. All the calls that were the stuff of legends. Bill had been there.

In the winter of 1977, I had been out of Rookie school almost five months and working with the best at the busiest house in the department; I'd learned a lot. Still, I didn't feel a part of the team. I wasn't really sure if I had it in me. The fire service is tough. The actual work is hard but that's not the real problem. It's the stress. You see it all. A family staring at a burned out, still smoking pile of char that used to be their home. The look in a father's eyes when he sees his only daughter, bloody and still, as you pull her from a mangled car. A junkie who has taken his last breath still holding the needle, and worse.

I just didn't know if I was cut out for the work. What if we ran a call and it was somebody I knew? What if I got seriously hurt at a fire? Could I handle it? People all around me, like Big Bill, seemed unfazed. Just another day at the office.

I shrugged off the vague uncertainty and went to the bay to load my bunker gear on the rig. D-Bird Johnson from the off-going shift was hanging his gear on the rack when the tones rang and the radio blared, "Engine 5, Engine 9, Ladder 9, Medic 9, Battalion 2 respond to a signal 33 at 866 Belmont Avenue. Caller reports smoke."

A structure fire. I thought the address was in an apartment complex about two miles away. I was right. After jumping into my gear and grabbing the rail on the tailboard, the bright red Pirsch pumper slid down the ramp and into traffic. With a blast of the air horn and the Sentry Siren winding up, we turned north. So much for the uncooked breakfast still on the counter.

Riding the board is an art. It's hard on the best of days to hang on as the engine careens around corners and hurriedly parts traffic. That day, the temperature was well below freezing and the sleet-laden wind whipped across the hose bed and blasted my face. It was brutal.

The vast majority of fire calls are false alarms and I had been to my share. As I clung to the crossbar and frantically fastened the final latches on the old cotton bunker coat the department had issued me a few months earlier, I thought this would be no different, just wetter. Then I saw it. Stretching skyward in the dim light ahead was a column of black smoke with a dark red glow at the base. A working fire.

I had been to smaller fires and some other serious calls but this would be the first major structure fire I had seen. My training had been comprehensive but nothing really prepares you for that first big fire. Clinging to a careening fire engine in rough weather, I found it especially difficult to prepare myself for the unknown. I tried to gather my wits as fear began to take hold. I took a few deep breaths. One of the senior firefighters had given me that tip early on. It fills the lungs with oxygen, preparing you for the first few minutes on scene. It also gives you a sense of control over the situation, forcing the rising fear to subside. I was delighted to find it actually working.

We slammed to a stop in front of a two-story apartment building with heavy smoke billowing from the back. A few residents, lightly dressed and shivering in the cold, scattered to allow us access to the building.

In a situation like this, it's the officer on the first-in engine who decides how the fire will be fought. This is based on basic priorities: Life first, always. Property second, if you can. At this time of the morning there was a good chance that not everyone was out of the building. So when Big Bill came around the engine and yelled *Mask up!* I knew we would be entering and searching the building even before Sergeant Jamie Butler, our driver and pump operator, laid and charged our attack lines. Entering a burning building without a charged nozzle was, and still is, extremely dangerous. Procedures changed later in my career to make initial search safer, but at that time we were expected to jump right in.

While Jamie stretched the first 1½" attack lines, I grabbed a Scott SCBA from its cumbersome green box in a compartment on the side of the engine. The Self Contained Breathing Apparatus would give me the fresh air needed to work in the smoky environment. Throwing it over my head, I adjusted straps as the pack landed on my back. Helmet and facemask grabbed, I met Big Bill at the entrance to the stairwell inside the breezeway on the first floor.

"Mask up and follow me," Bill's voice rumbled through his facepiece as he bounded up the stairs.

Seconds later, on the second-floor landing, Big Bill grabbed my shoulder, pushed me left, and yelled, "Clear that apartment." He turned and kicked the door to the right and entered the fire apartment.

On air, I cinched my black plastic helmet down, pulled my red rubber coated gloves tighter, and kicked the door near the lock just like they had trained me in Rookie school. It didn't budge. I hit it again — hard. This time it swung open with a loud crash and hot, black smoke billowed out.

I fell to my knees to get under the worst of the heat and began crawling inside. I used a left-hand search pattern. That meant keeping my left hand on the wall and feeling around, trying to find anyone who might be inside. I yelled a few times just in case someone was still asleep. Probably not, but it was possible. I couldn't see a thing. You almost never can. All those movies and TV shows try to give an accurate picture but they never show the smoke. If they did, that's all you would ever see. The reality is blackness.

I felt the heat on my neck and ears and tried to get lower. In those days we didn't wear hoods. The thinking then was that a person would monitor the heat with their ears and know when it was getting bad.

As I crawled hurriedly toward the first bedroom I remembered a story I had heard a few days before. Seems a lieutenant in a nearby department had risen up to try and see over a sofa. Evidently, the smoke was still manageable. The tips of his ears were burned in an instant. He required plastic surgery. The night before the procedure the crew gave him a New Ears Eve party.

Gaining the first bedroom I heard a faint voice. At first I thought it might be someone trapped but, as I stopped to hear clearer, I knew it was Big Bill screaming through his mask. "Rook. Come back. It's further along than I thought. Rook."

That sounded like an excellent idea. I turned and yelled loud, "On my way." If anything the smoke had dropped even lower and the heat was almost unbearable. I made my way back using my right hand on the wall.

I met Big Bill on the landing. As we turned to descend the stairs, I heard a deafening crash and felt a mighty push as smoke and searing heat erupted behind us. We tumbled down the stairs to the first landing. Bill helped me stand and we eventually made it outside. I ripped my mask off and looked up to see the entire roof structure had fallen into the apartments we had just left.

Looking back, I caught Bill's eye. We both knew how close we had come and I knew, instantly and without a doubt, he had saved my life. He nodded, smiled, and turned back to where the second-in crew, who had secured a water supply, were hurriedly playing water on the flames.

"Help Jamie get his connections to the ladder," he said without turning. "We'll need the master streams on this one." The moment was over and we would never broach the subject again. About that time, Battalion Chief Anders arrived on-scene and took command. Bill made his report and then took me to the rear to work a hand line to protect the nearest exposed building.

The fire lasted almost three hours and, thankfully, no one was injured. Everyone had gotten out before we got there.

During overhaul, Lieutenant O'Neal from the Inspection and Arson Investigation division found the remains of two road flares just inside the rear of the structure. Arson. Fire had run the back wall to the attic. An accidental fire is one thing but to almost die in a fire that some damn jackass had set was hard to take.

The next question was why. There are many reasons for arson; Lieutenant O'Neal explores them all. One of the police officers on-scene gave him one more to think about. It seemed that at the time of the fire, a convenience store was robbed at gunpoint a few miles away. Police response was hindered because nearby units were working traffic and crowd control at our fire.

An armed robbery in broad daylight was very unusual. Did someone set the fire to distract the police? Only time would tell.

We were the last to leave the scene. In those days it was first in, last out. Back at the station, after a quick break, we began the task of getting the apparatus back in service. Cleaning tools, fueling the engine, and giving our gear a quick clean was just the beginning. The hard job was relacing the truck. Clean, dry cotton-jacketed hose replaced what we had used at the fire. Awkward, heavy, and hard to pack, it was the bane of every firefighter. Later that afternoon, we would wash and place the used hose in the large, blue hose dryer at the back of the bay.

Fortunately, we had help. Big Bill's younger brother, Brandon, was at the station. He dropped by from time to time to visit. Sometimes he'd eat with us. Other times, like that day, he'd help us get back in service.

Ordinarily, we return to the fireground to check the scene. This is to ensure that the fire is truly out and no rekindle has occurred. Structure fires often rekindle when some out of the way hot spot, missed during the overhaul operations, gradually grows. Lieutenant O'Neal stayed on the scene for several hours and would be able to alert us of any problems. Thankfully, it wasn't necessary on this one.

It was almost two o'clock before we finally had a chance to eat. No one wanted to cook the forgotten breakfast so Brandon went out and got burgers. By the time he returned, we were on the road again. As the truck cleared the ramp, I clung to the crossbar and threw my arm through my wet bunker coat. Those burgers sure would've hit the spot.

This time it was a false alarm; inconvenient with food on the way but very typical. We returned to cold burgers. Brandon had left them on the kitchen counter. All things considered, man, they were pretty good.

After washing hose we finally got to sit for a few minutes and talk about the earlier fire. Big Bill compared it to other fires he had worked and Jamie told us how the initial hose lays had been done and the problems the other crews had getting the water supply established. Lieutenant O'Neal dropped by and the subject changed to the flares and the possibility that they had been a diversion to the police. He interviewed the occupants and the complex manager and told us that nothing else was apparent so far. He also said that the police were taking the idea seriously.

Jamie had just started a pot of chili when the radio cracked the air again. "Engine 5, Medic 9. Respond to a signal 41-I; Grant and Fifth."

That's a vehicle accident with possible injuries. You never know how bad it could be. In the few short months since Rookie class I had seen everything from a dented bumper to pure carnage. A vehicle accident can leave you with memories that are hard to put behind you.

We weaved our way through stopped traffic and beat Med 9 to the scene. A late model, blue Ford sat in the intersection with damage in the right rear. A brown Buick with a crushed front end sat nearby. There was a small crowd of people around the Buick.

As I came off the tailboard in the light rain, Big Bill bellowed from near the cab, "Make 'em safe, Rook." At any accident scene it's important to check for leaking gas and disconnect the batteries to prevent a spark or the possibility that something unexpected will occur. I heard about one scene where they were removing a victim and the car cranked in gear and lurched about five feet before ramming a telephone pole.

I pulled a wrench and screwdriver from the pocket of my bunker coat and hurried over to the Ford; I had taken to carrying them close for just such calls. Big Bill and Jamie, after glancing at the empty Ford, went to the Buick to check for injuries. Medic 9 topped the hill, weaved between a bus and three or four cars, and spotted near the police cruiser.

There were no gas leaks and the batteries proved uneventful. Sergeant Nichols, the paramedic on Med 9, told me to get their stretcher and, when I returned, they were applying a cervical collar to an elderly woman who had hit the windshield and was disoriented. She was the only one injured. The driver of the Ford was talking quietly with Officer Billows near his car.

It was short work getting Medic 9 on its way to the hospital. A wrecker arrived and latched on to the Buick; we pushed the Ford into a nearby parking lot. The wrecker driver and I swept glass and debris from the roadway.

The radio had been busy as we worked. I climbed back on the board and heard the dispatcher tell us to report to Station 2 for coverage. This could only mean that other units were engaged at a major call.

We were close to Station 2 before I saw it — another column of black smoke rising in the cold, wet air. There was a chance we would be sent to the fire to assist but, as I continued to watch the smoke, we pulled up to Station 2 and backed down the weatherbeaten concrete ramp. I climbed down and raised the old, wooden bay door to let Jamie get the rig out of the weather.

Inside the station we monitored the fire on the radio. It sounded like they had a knock down and were beginning to overhaul the scene. It was a mini-warehouse and would take some time. We took a few minutes for a snack and a Coke.

The station was the oldest in the department and it showed. Paint thickened the concrete block walls holding up a flat tar roof. Tiny rooms told of the lean years at the start of the department. I just shook my head and thanked the powers that be that I hadn't been stationed there. When I made it back to the day room, Big Bill grinned and said, "We should probably help Jack and the boys out a bit. Let's get the relace ready for them. I'm sure they would do it for us."

I looked at Jamie as he rolled his eyes and stood. More hose work. Bill grinned as the three of us began unrolling fresh hose for Engine 2.

As we were finishing, Battalion Chief Anders stopped by on his way from the fire to headquarters. He looked grim as we discussed our earlier fire. Then he dropped the bomb. Lieutenant O'Neal had found flares at the mini-warehouse. On top of that, another robbery had occurred a few miles away at the same time. The police were determined to catch the perpetrator and had told the Fire Chief to expect fewer officers at fire scenes until they found a way to stop him.

After he left we talked about it for a few minutes. This meant we would have to be more careful at fire scenes. Without police presence traffic and bystanders would be more of a problem. Big Bill ran his fingers through his thinning hair and mused, "Might as well buckle in and get comfortable. Sounds like he ain't finished. I guess this shift's gonna' be a long one."

When they released Engine 2 we headed back home. After a quick wash and dry for the engine, we had chili for supper and were able to relax a few hours before bed.

After making my bunk and crawling inside, I tried to sleep. There were three of us in that bunkroom and at least two of us were world-class snorers. The last thing I remember before sleep overtook me was the heat and blackness of that apartment just before the roof fell in.

Climbing on the tailboard and fastening my coat I woke enough to realize we were headed to another fire. It's funny how, when you're new to the life, you worry about not waking up and missing a call. Then, after a few long nights, you realize the truth. You're part of a team, part of that big truck out there, and where it goes, you go. Even when you're asleep.

This time we were headed to a structure fire over in Three's area. We would be backup. Our assignment would probably involve securing a water source before actually fighting fire.

I glanced at my watch. 3:12 a.m. No rest for the weary. At least the rain had stopped but it was still cold and wet. I took deep breaths and prepared to work but, as we arrived on-scene, it became obvious that Engine 3's crew had made a quick knock down and we wouldn't need a water supply.

Light smoke still clung to the abandoned house in the dim spotlight from Engine 3. Patrol cars were absent and I remembered what was said earlier. Big Bill told me to stay with the rig while he and Jamie moved around their engine and found Lieutenant Jefferson dropping his pack on the asphalt. He had the remains of a dirty, red flare in his hand.

I climbed inside the cab to get warm as the radio crackled to life. Lieutenant Jefferson was canceling all units that weren't on-scene with the exception of the on-call arson investigator. Everyone in the department now knew or suspected that our arsonist had struck again.

A couple of minutes later the radio blared again. Dispatch was calling us to see if we could respond. Before I could react, I saw Big Bill jump into the cab of Engine 3 and respond. We were dispatched, with Medic 9 again, to a signal 50.

Gunshot. Police were on scene at an overnight market not three miles away.

I fell out of the cab as Jamie and Bill ran up. "Hey, looks like they caught the bastard," Bill grinned as he swung into the cab. I scrambled onto the tailboard just as the engine dropped in gear. Truth be known, I couldn't wait to see the lowlife that had been causing so much trouble.

Flashing blue lights were visible from two blocks away. As we pulled up it was obvious that every police unit within miles had responded. About eight or ten patrol cars were there. I even saw the K9 unit near the small convenience store at the center of the action.

Jamie spotted the engine about a hundred yards short of the building and, as I stepped from the board and Jamie was setting the brake, I saw Big Bill headed down to the scene. I dropped my coat on the tailboard, grabbed our first aid kit, and followed. About twenty yards in I saw three officers around the open trunk of a red Toyota that sat partially off the road against a tree. As I passed the Toyota, my eyes were drawn to the trunk by a camera flash. I saw a small box of road flares, about half empty. No doubt. This was the arsonist all right.

Further down the road I saw a skinny guy handcuffed in the back of a patrol car. He didn't look hurt. The fact that he wasn't shot should have alerted me. It didn't. I turned to tell Jamie they had got him. He was just leaving the engine but something wasn't right. As he ran by me he choked out, "Jesus, Rook."

I spun around. In the light from the storefront I saw Bill on his knees over a figure on the ground. Three or four cops were standing around with their backs to him. Something wasn't right. Then it hit me. Red Toyota. I didn't want to believe what was happening but I began running anyway.

When I got there Big Bill Carson was crying into his hands, moaning, "Oh God, Oh God." Jamie was beside him, bending over the body of Brandon Carson, Bill's younger brother. Blood covered part of his shirt and the side of his head. After checking for any sign of life, Jamie looked at Bill and shook his head slowly. There was no doubt he was gone.

I knelt beside Bill, hand on his shoulder. He turned to me, his eyes still streaming, and tried to talk. Nothing came out.

Jamie and I held him until Battalion Chief Anders took him to his car. By that time Med 9 was there. Sergeant Nichols sat with Bill and the Chief until the State Patrol took photos and released the body. They were called in because it was an officer-related shooting. We were able to load Brandon for the trip to the hospital to be pronounced. Chief

Anders followed them slowly down the street with Big Bill still in the car.

Jamie and I remained on-scene doing what little we could to assist the police. We set up temporary floodlights and parked the rig to help keep bystanders away. Beyond that we did little but sit on the tailboard too stunned to talk and watched as they completed their investigation.

The officer in question, Joey Cummings, sat in the back of Police Lieutenant Sam Holbrook's cruiser. For most of the time he sat quietly staring ahead. Twice I saw him turn away and bury his face in his hands. The only thing I knew about Joey was that he had gone to high school with Big Bill.

We were finally released and returned to the station just a few minutes before shift change. Everyone on the oncoming shift already knew but they still wanted details. I just listened as Jamie quietly answered their questions.

I was about to pull away from the small parking area at the station when Jamie stopped me.

"Tough night," he said looking around. "So, I'll see you next shift?"

Caught off-guard I muttered, "Yeah. See you then."

As I drove home, I wasn't so sure. It was a lot to take in and I wasn't at all sure I would be back. I thought I'd make a decision after a long sleep and more time to think.

My decision was delayed when Chief Walker phoned me at home later that day. He told me to take the next shift off with pay and not to report for work until after the funeral. He assured me he had told Bill and Jamie the same. We talked about the situation and he expressed his regret. After the call I just shook my head. I couldn't believe I rated a call from the Chief of the department.

Four days later, I pulled into the funeral home wondering if I would even see Bill. I felt like an outsider because I didn't know any of his family save Brandon and Bill, and I really didn't know them well.

I was stunned to find an array of department vehicles stacked in the lot. Three engines, a ladder truck, two Medic units, and about five or six cars lined the back of the lot. The rest was filled with private vehicles. I had to park in an open field beside the home.

Inside were most of the people I knew from work along with many others I had heard about but didn't know. In my mind I compared the turnout to a funeral I had recently attended for my uncle, a career union plumber. Four friends from work had shown up.

I'm sure there were a large group of family members there too. I did see Bill beside the casket and spoke to him briefly. He stood quietly shaking hands and introducing his mother, who was silent and just nodded and tried to smile as the parade of people filed by.

After about half an hour the crowd suddenly went silent. I turned toward the door and saw people slowly parting to reveal Joey Cummings, the officer who shot Brandon, standing alone. He and Bill locked eyes and, after a long, breathless pause, Bill led his mother across the room.

Not a word was spoken before Bill wrapped his arms around Joey and began to sob openly. Joey broke down too. Then Bill's mother led them to a grouping of chairs in the far corner of the room.

Conversation resumed without comment from anyone. It may have been the most awkward moment I had ever witnessed and surely the most humbling.

The actual service was anticlimactic. I remember a few words of the Pastor and the music was inspiring. Bill and his family followed the casket to the graveside and most of us joined them for a few quick words. I slipped away not much later. I still had more than a full day to clear my mind and make a decision.

When I pulled my truck into the small parking space beside the diesel pump behind the station two days later I was more confused than ever. I didn't know how I could stay and I surely didn't know how I could quit. I grabbed the bag holding my food and sundries for the shift, zipped my jacket, and trudged across the lot in a strong wind.

It was warm inside. I cleared the door of the day room and saw Jamie cooking breakfast, Big Bill reading the morning paper, and a few of the guys from the other shift making ready to leave. The cool green walls and the tattered furniture suddenly felt like home.

I looked up and Bill was watching me over his coffee. He grinned and said, "Ready to save the world, Rook?"

I looked around the room and smiled self-consciously "You bet, Lieutenant."

The radio came to life. Everyone laughed. We began another shift.

Steve Farmer, a true jack of all trades and master of none, is a fire department Battalion Chief, retired, and now a real estate investor living in McDonough, Georgia, who plays harp guitar and writes songs. The first thing Steve wrote got published in The Reader's Digest. He is now three-for-three.

facebook.com/steve.farmer.330

Married in Haste

Deborah Lacy

Sarah loved Max in a way she'd never loved anyone before. When he put the engagement ring on her finger, she felt giddy. But after a week at the beach with Max and Max's former police partner and his wife, she was ready to go home.

Max kept sending her off with Magnolia while he and Eddie went golfing. And while she found herself to be extremely fond of Magnolia Clearwater, this wasn't the vacation she'd expected. Now here she was again on a sunrise beach walk with Magnolia while the guys took in an early bird tee time on a nearby golf course. Max said it was important. He had promised to make it up to her. He asked her to trust him.

She was trying.

Walking down the beach, her perfectly manicured toes sinking in the sand, Magnolia said, "No one is ever what they seem at first. It can take years to truly know someone."

Sarah twisted the engagement ring around her finger and looked up at the older woman almost in defiance. "I know what you're trying to say. But really, he told me everything and we've moved past it."

"And you're sure you're OK with it?" Magnolia said.

"Just because you've been married four times doesn't make you an expert." That was rude and Sarah was sorry as soon as the words left her lips. "He promised it would never happen again."

"Forgive me, I shouldn't have stuck my nose in. It's just I see a little of myself in you. I was shy and tentative when I was younger. Didn't speak up for myself. If you don't learn how to take care of yourself, a relationship can drown you."

"I can't imagine that."

"Sarah, you have to take control. Just because you said yes to an engagement doesn't mean you have to marry him. Engagements are a time for further reflection. You know what they say, 'Marry in haste, repent at leisure'."

"We're past it."

The older woman smiled again. "It's your life. Live it how you want. Just make sure it is what *you* want."

The cold made her shiver. She zipped her jacket up to the top and pulled the collar over her chin.

"You're cold," Magnolia said, "Let's go back and get some coffee. It'll be warmer up off the beach. We can walk back on the road."

Sarah nodded and followed Magnolia down the beach toward a little wooden bridge that went over the sweetgrass to the road. But as they got closer, they could see a large brown heap on the sand.

"What is that?" Magnolia said, pointing her finger toward the heap.

"It looks like a seal," Sarah said. "Maybe it needs help."

"I don't think we have seals here on Pawleys Island," Magnolia answered.

"Let's go check it out."

"If you feel that we must, Sugar."

As they got closer, it became clear the heap wasn't a seal.

A woman. Lay dead. On the beach. Her head was bloody. Her face contorted.

"Call 911!" Sarah called as she ran toward her as fast as possible; the loose sand slowed her down with every step. When Sarah reached the body, she felt the woman's wrist for a pulse but found none.

"They're on their way," Magnolia yelled through the wind, walking briskly in Sarah's direction. "I called Eddie. He said to stay here until they arrive."

Sarah looked at the woman lying on the beach and felt a pitch in her stomach. With a rumble, her breakfast announced that it did not plan on staying where it was. She walked away from the body quickly and managed to get to the surf before she threw up. A wave came and washed it all away.

"Sugar? Are you OK? You're not pregnant or anything, right?"

Sarah shook her head. "I've...I've never seen a dead body before."

"It's good for you to know what Max goes through when he sees a dead body. Happens to him several times a week and he doesn't get sick. Look at this as an opportunity. Something we can experience together with our men."

Sarah couldn't understand how Magnolia could possibly be trying to turn this situation into relationship lemonade, especially since two minutes ago she was saying she shouldn't marry Max.

A group of people, seven men, women, and teenagers in jeans and sweatshirts, were headed their way on the beach, not twenty feet away.

"We can't let them see this," Sarah said.

"Probably shell seekers. Pawleys Island is famous for its shells. They'll turn around."

"They aren't turning around."

The group walked toward them with excitement, cellphone cameras clicking away. A man in khaki pants seemed to be in charge. He was wearing a sweatshirt that said "Pawleys Island Ghost Tours".

Sarah walked toward them carefully, keeping herself between the tour group and the body on the beach. "I'm sorry. This part of the beach is closed," she said with as much authority as she could muster. "You'll have to leave immediately."

The leader spoke up, "We were called about a potential ghost sighting and we came to check it out."

"Is she really dead?" a woman asked. "Or is this another fake?"

"It would be ever so helpful if you all could take some pictures," the tour guide said.

"How is that helpful?" Sarah whispered to Magnolia. "I thought Eddie said not to let anyone near her. They'll mess up the scene."

But as the two women talked, the tourists started snapping photos.

"Everyone should stop taking photos at once," Magnolia said.

"Or just leave. That's better. Everyone leave," Sarah said. But the crowd ignored her.

"So," said a teenaged girl said talking through her braces, "will this woman become a ghost?"

The man wearing the Ghost Tours sweatshirt answered the teenage girl's question as if this were a Halloween fun house instead of a real body. "Hard to say. She was taken in her prime, and that's step one. Looks like foul play, and that's step two. Step three is a need for revenge. And that's what we don't know."

"The gash on her head tells me she needs revenge," the teenage boy said.

"Please leave," Sarah said, trying again. "We need this area clear. The police are on their way."

A bald man turned to Sarah. "Oh don't worry. It's not a real body. Everything on this tour is fake. Ask him to show you the phony ghost pictures on his phone. Claims a bunch of blurry lights proves there's paranormal activity." The man rolled his eyes. "It's been almost ten minutes since the last stupid trick. I can't believe this tour cost us thirty bucks apiece."

A little blonde girl grabbed the bag of shells lying next to the body and riffled through it.

"Put that down!" Sarah moved toward the girl and took it away from her.

"Nothing good in there anyway," the girl said. "No shark teeth. No Pawleys Island shells. The Pawleys shells are good luck. I have three."

"Please, please, please. Move away from the body," Sarah tried again.

She turned to see Eddie and Max running down the beach headed for them, kicking up sand as they went. Eddie went straight for the body. Her fiancé went straight for her.

"I'm so sorry you had to see this," Max said, hugging her. She felt safe and warm in his arms.

"I tried to keep everyone away but they took photos," she said. Her stomach lurched and she thought she might have to throw up again.

"I am Eddie Chandler, with the Pawleys Island Police," he said with a Jersey accent that cut through the wind. "I need this area clear. Now."

There were sounds of disappointment from the crowd.

"Was she killed by a vengeful ghost, do you think?" a teenage boy asked. "There are a lot of ghosts on this island. The Grey Man. Theodosia. The Pink Lady. Anyone of them could have done it."

"This isn't an episode of Scooby Doo," Max said, clearly annoyed. "Please move along."

"They took pictures," Sarah told the guys. "Lots and lots of pictures."

Eddie sighed. "Listen up. I need everyone to give me their electronic devices, now."

"I'm not giving anyone this phone."

"I need my camera."

"This is not a request." He took off his jacket and put it in the sand. "Put your devices down on the jacket now." He turned to Max. "Can you record which device belongs to which person?"

Max nodded.

One by one the tourists put their cameras and cellphones on top of Eddie's jacket as instructed.

"When will we get them back?" asked the man.

"Contact the Pawleys Island Police Department on Monday."

"But we're on vacation."

"And this woman is dead," Eddie said.

Eddie, Magnolia, and Sarah moved closer to the body, leaving Max to negotiate with the crowd. The three looked down at her.

"Man, they made a mess of the scene," Eddie said in a gruff voice. "Footprints everywhere. We don't even know what they destroyed. And this

retirement job was supposed to be boring —
nothing but breaking up loud beach parties."

"The paramedics are taking their time," Sarah
said.

"I called them off, once I confirmed that she
was dead," Eddie said. "This isn't Newark. We
don't have the resources they do. Don't want to
take an ambulance away from someone who could
be saved."

Magnolia walked over to the body, her skirt
swaying the in the wind, her feet making the
smallest of footprints in the sand.

"She does look familiar to me but I can't quite
place her," Magnolia said. "Do you recognize her,
Max? Eddie?"

Magnolia paused and looked at Max and then
Eddie, waiting for them to respond.

"I know who she is!" Magnolia said as she
snapped her fingers. "Dolly Wainwright. Her beach
house has all those Palmetto trees out front. Max,
didn't you hook up with her last summer when
you came down to help Eddie move here?"

Sarah looked at Max with raised eyebrows.
Max shrugged his shoulders. This was Dolly. The
woman he'd slept with, cheated on her with, and
now she was dead.

Max knelt down and looked more closely at the woman's face. "That's Dolly," he said gruffly.

Eddie's face turned red in a way Sarah had never seen before now. She couldn't tell if he was embarrassed or mad. Was he embarrassed for Max? Magnolia smiled a stupid I-told-you-so smile.

Sarah decided to let Eddie know she knew about Max's shameful secret. It would come out anyway.

"Eddie. Max slept with her. I knew before we got engaged. We were broken up for a few weeks. I don't like it, but I'm OK with it."

Max didn't say anything.

"They were broken up, Eddie," said Magnolia. "And Sarah's OK with it. Sarah — are you OK with Dolly being dead?"

"No, of course not."

"Max — did you tell Eddie that you slept with Dolly? Or don't best friends talk about their affairs?"

"Magnolia," Max said, "this isn't helpful. A woman is dead. We can talk about the personal side later."

Magnolia said, "But if this was any other case, Max, you'd be interested in who the victim slept with, and if you're not interested, then my first question as a detective would be: Why aren't you interested. Isn't that your first question, Eddie?"

With his glove-covered hand, Eddie reached down next to the woman's head and pulled up a piece of gold metal.

"It's a bracelet," he said.

"This looks like the bracelet I gave you for your birthday, Sarah," Max said.

Max moved closer to get a better look.

"It's even got the heart charm with your initials on it."

"It must have fallen off when you checked her pulse," Magnolia said.

"I wasn't wearing it," Sarah said. "I couldn't find it this morning."

Magnolia moved closer to Sarah and whispered, "Tell them you were wearing the bracelet when we found her."

"A woman has been murdered," Sarah said, refusing to whisper. "I'm not lying about a bracelet."

Eddie looked up at her as if he'd heard. He stared at her as if he was trying to read her thoughts.

"What's the matter?" she asked him.

"Maybe Sarah and I should go get our nails done while you two work," Magnolia said, putting her hand on Sarah's arm.

"No," Max and Eddie said at once and then looked at one another like an old married couple sharing a secret. Sarah wondered if she and Max would ever be that close.

Eddie stood up and brushed bits of sand from his pant legs and put himself between Sarah and Magnolia. "Until we catch this killer, the two of you aren't going out of our sight."

Max caught Sarah's gaze. He was trying to communicate with her wordlessly, like he did with Eddie, but she didn't understand. Not yet. But she nodded as if she did.

Her stomach lurched again. She needed space. She turned her back to them and walked a few steps toward the water. And there she saw it. A seashell sticking out of the sand. It had bigger grooves, going sideways instead of the usual up and down. It was what they called the Pawleys Island shell. The little girl had said it meant good luck, but surely that was just a tale. She picked it up and put it in the pocket of her sweat jacket. No use turning down good luck when your favorite bracelet has been found next to a dead body. Max came up behind her and put his hand on her shoulder.

Eddie breathed in deeply. "Those tourists sure trampled everything."

"Why would anyone want her dead?"

"Sugar, no one is suggesting Sarah killed her," said Magnolia.

"Why did you say that, Magnolia?" Max asked, putting his arm around his fiancé.

"Because her bracelet got here somehow, Max. Out here. On the beach. From the nightstand. In the guest room. Does anyone else have a key?"

Eddie answered, "I have a key. Magnolia, you have a key. We gave you two one key. That's it. With so many guns in the house, I had the locks changed when I moved in."

"Magnolia here was telling me just a few minutes ago that I need to take an interest in Max's work," Sarah said. "So, here's what I see. It's my bracelet by the body, taken from a locked house with three keys. The victim slept with my fiancé. And I led Magnolia here to the body."

"Finally! Sugar, you are starting to understand. Don't forget how you called the ghost tour company and told them to come directly here to the exact spot where the body lay. Such a creative plan to get all of that wonderful evidence destroyed. You made that phone call from your very own cellphone, which wasn't so smart. And if we don't move quickly, the police will find a note from you to Dolly warning her to stay away from Max."

"Magnolia," Eddie said. "This won't work."

"Of course it will, darling. I have thought of everything, as I always do. If you don't want Sarah to pay for your crime, Eddie, you will do exactly what I say for the rest of your life. Jail is a nasty place for a woman of quality. Why should she suffer?"

"Eddie didn't murder this woman," Sarah said.

"Oh, Sugar, of course he did. Dolly Wainright was as good as dead the day Eddie slept with her."

Sarah and Max turned to Eddie, who was staring at Magnolia with hatred. "Eddie slept with Dolly, too?" Sarah said.

"You are pretty, Sarah, but you're slow," said Magnolia.

"Our first step is to vow that none of us will ever mention finding Sarah's bracelet. Next I will go remove the note blaming Sarah from Dolly's house. Eddie will call the Murrells Inlet Police Department and transfer the case to them because he slept with the victim. Without the bracelet and the physical evidence, Sarah won't be a suspect. But if any of the three of you ever cross me again, I will retrieve my pile of retroactive evidence and make sure she goes directly to jail."

"This isn't happening," Sarah said.

"Magnolia? Did you really think that Max and I have been golfing twelve hours a day in this cold weather?" Eddie said. "That he'd spend two weeks of his precious vacation with you harping at his fiancé? No one will ever suspect Sarah had anything to do with this murder."

"Eddie, I do the talking now. You will remain silent until I address you."

"I don't think you understand, Magnolia," Max said. "We have our own pile of evidence. I got worried when you and Eddie got hitched so fast. I started looking into the unnatural deaths of your first three husbands. Those supposedly untraceable poisons you used aren't really untraceable. The medical examiner is working on the autopsies right now. Sarah's been keeping you busy while we had your first three husbands dug up."

Magnolia's eyes went wide with surprise. "What are you talking about?"

"I married a murderess," Eddie said. "Blinded by love. And we have the evidence to prove it."

Wordlessly, Magnolia turned her back to them and moved toward the ocean.

No one moved as she walked slowly into the chilly water one step at a time. First her feet got wet, then her skirt. Then her sweater, weighing her down.

The three watched as she walked deeper and deeper into the waves.

Deborah Lacy's short mystery fiction has appeared in numerous magazines and anthologies including Alfred Hitchcock's Mystery Magazine, Mystery Weekly, and an anthology for the world's largest mystery fan convention, Bouchercon.

She runs the Mystery Playground website and writes for MacMillan Publishing's CriminalElement.com blog.

deborahlacy.com
Facebook.com/deborah.lacy

STORIES OF SOUTHERN HUMOR and CRIME: ANTHOLOGY

Hunter Hunted

Claire Count

"I'm a-gonna kill him, Ma," said Fred. He grabbed the shotgun resting by the kitchen door and shoved a handful of paper-cased shells in his corduroy jacket pocket. "Be back soon."

Ma added a dab of water and kept on kneading the biscuit dough. "Oh? Who you gonna kill? Wanna take Alvin with you? Think he's round back choppin' wood or some such. Do him good to blow off some steam."

"Nyah, I got this. It's a personal matter." He looked on the hook by the door for the car key. "Ma, where's the key to the Studebaker?"

She threw some flour on the breadboard and started rolling out the biscuits. "That's right, your brother Doc wanted to go check out that bank in Deland. He'll be back before dinner. You can trust him to be on time to eat." She laughed at her own joke. "Can it wait?"

"I suppose." Crestfallen, he leaned the shotgun against the cabinet. He pulled an RC Cola out of the icebox. The steel bottle opener seemed tiny in his meaty hands. The cap fell to the floor and rolled under the sink.

Ma had finished up her biscuits when she thought she heard sobbing. "Fred, honey, is something wrong?" She removed her apron and hung it on a nail.

He sniffed. "You'll think I'm silly. And maybe it is silly, but I loved that dog."

Her brows furrowed in concern. "What happened?" She cleaned the dough from her hands in the sink and sat at the table.

"Okkie was a good dog. He was a mutt, but I kinda am a mutt too, so we got along good. He shoulda stayed home. Why did the dog have to go bark at old Joe? Joe killed him, and now I'm gonna kill Joe!"

"You sure about that? That Joe killed Okkie?"

"Okkie didn't come for breakfast this morning so I went looking for him. I found his collar with a lot of blood on it over where Joe lives. You know over near where I used to take him duck huntin'. Dog went trespassing and *SNAP!* Now he's a goner." His voice trembled.

"Joe is a tough cookie. You sure you want to wrestle with him? Been around a long time. He knows these parts, better than we do. You'd be on his home turf."

"Ma, he killed mah dog!" he bellowed in grief.

"OK, OK. Let's do this right, though." She stepped out the porch and called out. "Herm, Alvin, I need your help please."

A few minutes later they came in. Alvin grabbed a beer from the Electrolux fridge. Herm was covered in a layer of summer sweat, so he washed off in the sink. "Those biscuits smell good, Ma." Herman smacked his lips. "I woulda killed for some of your home cookin' when I was in the big house."

"Well, if you boys go and help Fred out quick, you can be back before the dinner is done."

Alvin let out a big belch and tossed the empty bottle in the rubbish bin. "I'm in. What's up?"

Fred ran the back of his sleeve across his face. Not manly to cry. "Joe killed Okkie. I am aiming for some hard revenge."

"I'm sorry, Fred. Okkie was a good hound. Let's just get a new one. Leave ol' Joe alone. We're tryin' to lay low."

"No. We get a new one and the dog wanders and *BAM!* He'll be a goner, too. I wanna take him out and take him out hard. Roll his body into the swamp so nobody never finds him."

"Kid's gotta point. Let's get Tommy and have some fun. Joe lives out in the marsh near the lake.

Nobody will be nearby to hear us." Alvin went to the door and fetched his mud boots.

Herm worried, but knew that look in Alvin's eyes. Alvin just plain liked to kill. "Tommy is a little loud, don't you think?" He headed upstairs to change into a clean shirt.

"Sometimes, you have to use the right tool for the job," winked Alvin as he went into the living room. Resting atop the polished piano were two Tommy guns and a dozen or so ammo drums.

"You guys are da best," grinned Fred and pulled on his high waders.

"Back in a bit, Ma. Need us to get anything while we're out?" Herm leaned over to give her a peck on the cheek.

"Not really. But if you happen to see Mrs. Johnson, see if you could buy another jar of her strawberry preserves. Someone in this house eats it like it's going out of style." She shot Fred a wink.

"If we see her," Herm promised, hoping they weren't going to be seeing anyone. "Alright, Fred, lead the way to Joe's place."

"We are gonna have to walk. Doc is out with the car, again," groused Fred.

"Ain't far. Let's go git it done," grinned Alvin. He lit a Lucky Strike and took a draw then put on his grey linen jacket and grabbed his fedora. "Ain't his lucky day."

Herm slipped on his jacket and adjusted his tie. He took a Tommy gun and drum from Alvin with a thank-you nod. "Alright, let's do it. Keep dinner warm for us, Ma."

As always, Ma gave Herm and Fred a kiss before they headed out. With their wild lifestyle, she never knew when it would be the last time she saw them. She nodded at Alvin, Fred's friend. "Don't take too long. No one likes tough chicken."

After a volley of *yes ma'ams*, the trio went off hunting.

"This way." Fred took point.

"You know this won't bring Okkie back?" Herm tried one last time.

"Yeah, but it will make me feel better." Fred rested the shotgun against his shoulder. "And think about it this way, we'll be doing a social service to protect everyone else's pets. Joe is just a mean ol' son of a bitch that needs puttin' down. I'm gonna enjoy whackin' him."

"Alright. If that's the way you want it."

Herman had a bad feeling about this. Come down to it, he had a bad feeling about moving to Florida at all. He cursed under his breath as a strand of Spanish moss smacked into his face. The trio crossed out of the wetland forest into the freshwater marsh. Tromping through the bulrushes trying to find firm ground, he regretted not changing into high wader boots like the others.

Dusk arrived and mosquitoes were in full flight as they reached Joe's place. The crickets' loud whine was interrupted only by bullfrogs' calls as they splashed through the muck. From a tussock, a flock of birds erupted into the air, irritated at being disturbed.

"Come on, Joe. We wanna talk to you," Fred yelled, his hatred palpable.

"Come out, come out, wherever you are," taunted Alvin in singsong.

Ol' Joe was not afraid. He was hungry; he was always hungry. Floating low, only his eyes above water, he studied the men. His eyes were piercing steel looking for a point of weakness. He found it. He chose his mark. His powerful tail thrust him forward underwater.

"Anyone see him?" The men moved together. Something instinctual told them they were no longer the hunter here.

A movement in the cattails was the only warning. Joe charged forward. In his natural element, he was the alpha predator, and these fools were prey. His head came out of the water as he snapped at the intruders. Fred fell into the marsh as he dodged the attack. His shotgun fell into the water, useless now, paper-cased shells ruined. Alvin spun the Tommy gun around to fire. Herm knocked the gun up so it fired into the air. More birds shot up, squawking in alarm.

"What you do that for?" Alvin yelled.

"You coulda hit Fred," barked Herman. "He's too close."

Joe hissed and lunged. He did not get this big by avoiding risks and easy meal tickets. His mouth opened wide, ready to snap any limb he could. That left leg would be mighty tasty. His massive mandible and yellowed teeth were made for crushing. He was big and mean and he liked it. Maybe he could grab him and drag him into the lake, drown him, and have him later, after the waters had tenderized him. The gator circled under the water and struck again.

Fred struggled to get back on his feet. The soft mud held him down, giving way as he pushed against it. Almost like the marsh helped Joe. His hand touched something hard and familiar. He gripped it tightly. Fred picked up his shotgun and bashed its butt into Joe's nose. "Take this!" He pounded with all his strength because his life depended on it.

Joe stopped, stunned. Prey is not supposed to do that. The gator clawed into the human's leg. Ah! The sweet smell of blood. Joe crawled up Fred's body to push the man under water, hold him there.

Fred held his breath and pounded again and again. The gun cracked against the gator's snout. The shotgun butt split from the force of the blows.

Joe shook his head in pain and slipped away back into the murky water. There would be easier prey, safer prey. He slid into his nearby gator hole along the lake edge, to wait for another day.

Alvin let loose where the gator went under. Rata-ta-tat! No blood. "Don't think we got him."

Herm came over and helped Fred up. Fred grinned. "That's OK. He won't mess with us again. I broke his nose real good."

"Yep, Ol' Gator Joe won't be messing with the Barker boys again." Herm patted his brother's back with relief. They were not going to live forever, not with their bank-robbing lifestyle, but at least no one died today.

* * * * *

"So the Barker boys and their buddy Alvin swaggered home and had a big dinner of chicken and biscuits," concluded Jimi with a theatrical bow; her dark hair tumbled across her face.

Luis laughed. "You are such a ham. You should have gone into acting after graduating from Florida State."

"Nyah, I'm too bossy," grinned the young stage manager.

"You know that's not how it actually happened." Luis looked at Gator Joe's preserved foot displayed in a prominent glass case. He cringed thinking of those black claws digging into someone.

"No? But a good story anyway," said Jimi Rey. "And Ma Barker really lived in a house nearby along the lake. Gator Joe caused their eventual downfall…and is how the FBI tracked them down. The state is converting the house into a museum, I think my abuela said."

"Your table is ready," said the collegiate server. He led the way to the patio overlooking Lake Weir.

"Here is to the crime that inspired my favorite hangout, Gator Joe's," Jimi said, lifting her glass.

"Hear! Hear!" toasted Luis. "To the lost Okkie of Ocklawaha."

Claire Count is one of those people who is always curious, always wanting to learn more. During a trip to Florida, she joined her family at Gator Joe's where she learned the story of the Barker Boys, inspiring *Hunter Hunted*. Life's little puzzles are often turned into mystery and suspense short stories and occasionally into poems.

Last year, Claire's first international publication was released by Black Hare Press in their dark drabble mystery collection *UNRAVEL*, on Amazon through Kindle Unlimited. A drabble is a short story of precisely 100 words.

A mystery in only 100 words was a challenge.

Claire's degrees in Theatre and Psychology give her insight to build dimensional, relatable characters. Claire has been a role-playing gamer since her teens, which shows in her imaginative but plausible fantasy works. A lifelong member of Sisters in Crime and former Atlanta chapter president, she sometimes speaks at writing conferences on mysteries and character building.

ClaireCount.com
Twitter @ClaireCount

The Rag

Mark Mellon

They drank cold orange squash under an umbrella's shade on the terrace.

"You let me win the last set, Jay."

"I was tired after the first two, Carleton. Now I owe you fifty."

"You can get it back at backgammon tonight."

Jayson Inslee sipped his drink. That was another thing Carleton Jannings liked about him: Unlike many Southerners, Inslee wasn't garrulous; he knew when to be quiet. Even though they'd only met two days ago, being with Inslee was already like enjoying an old friend's easy company.

The air was cool, with a fresh breeze from the Atlantic. White-jacketed waiters hustled past, bearing salvers heaped high with food and drink. Elegant men and women in holiday attire toyed with their orders or discreetly drank cocktails. Women darted curious glances at the two handsome young men. Jannings boldly smiled back only to have them duck behind fans.

Inslee took off his sunglasses. "You know, I think I recognize that car coming this way. Not too many gray Packards on the road."

A pearl-tinted '24 Packard Six drove down the clamshell road. It stopped before the hotel's sweeping pink marble staircase. A gray-uniformed chauffeur got out and opened a passenger door. A tall man got out, stout, elderly, in a white suit with a broad-brimmed straw hat. He walked up the stairs, slender cane at a rakish angle.

Inslee laughed. "I was right. Dog my cats if that isn't Colonel Thatcher, one of the richest men in Savannah."

"You know him?"

"Of course. My father does legal work for him. Both our families go way back in Savannah."

"Say, isn't that young Jayson Inslee?" Thatcher boomed, striding toward them. Inslee rose to shake hands, but Thatcher crushed him in a bear hug. "And who's this with you? What's your name, sir?"

Inslee made the introductions. "This is Carleton Jannings. Carleton, this is Colonel Barnwell Thatcher, last of the Georgia fire-eaters."

Thatcher shook hands with Jannings.

"Colonel. Please. Join us," Jannings said.

"Why, I don't mind if I do," he said.

Inslee got up and fetched Thatcher a chair. The old man settled in slowly, with an appreciative gasp. A waiter came and awaited his order.

Thatcher handed him five dollars, folded lengthwise. The waiter smiled and hurried off.

"What brings you to the Sanford Hotel, Colonel? Are you staying here? That would be a pleasant coincidence since I'm already a guest," Inslee said.

"No, I have a place at Opelika Bay when I have business in Florida. My appointment in Target City isn't until three. I thought a little pick-me-up might be in order while I waited. Ah, here it comes now."

The waiter placed a chilled silver mug before Thatcher. He smiled his thanks and took a deep draft of a fizzy, iced drink topped with white foam and a cherry.

"Ah, a Ramos Gin Fizz. You can still get them here, made New Orleans style. Would you boys care for one?" Inslee and Jannings politely declined. Thatcher shook his head at their folly and took another stiff belt. "So, Carleton. Tell me about yourself. Or, better yet, indulge an old man's fancy and let me guess. You're an Ivy League man. Am I right?"

"Why, yes—"

"No, wait. Let me be even more specific. You're a Yale man, aren't you? Fifty dollars to you right here if I'm wrong."

Carleton's eyes opened in surprise. "Keep your money, Colonel. Yes, Yale, '22. How did you know, if you don't mind my asking?"

"No real secret to it. I spent my younger days on Wall Street. I could tell a Dartmouth man from one who went to Cornell." Thatcher reached over and slapped Jannings lightly on the knee. "But I never got used to that vile stuff you Yankees call weather up there. That's the reason I came back to Savannah."

"The Colonel is clever, right, Carleton?" Inslee turned to Thatcher. "What brings you to Florida, Colonel? Are you thinking of buying land?"

Thatcher grimaced. "This Florida land boom is nothing but a bubble. Put your money in the market instead. That's my business today. I'm going to see Harry Easton." Thatcher turned to Inslee. "Do you know Harry?" Inslee shook his head. Thatcher continued. "Harry is the manager of the Orange Blossom Land and Investment Company. Very interesting fellow. Runs his own business even though he's barely thirty. Say, why don't you boys come along with me?"

Inslee shifted uncomfortably in his seat. "Colonel, we shouldn't intrude—"

Jannings waved an impatient hand at Inslee. "Oh, come on, Jay." He swiveled his head to

Thatcher. "I would love to go, Colonel. I've been thinking about becoming a broker. Either that or law school. This might help me decide."

Thatcher smiled patronizingly at Inslee. "You see, Jayson? Your own friend agrees with me. Why don't you boys clean up and change while I have another drink?"

"Well, all right, Colonel, if you really think we won't be in your way. I know how important a businessman you are."

"Oh, stuff and tosh, Jayson. Go get ready like I said while I relax here."

"All right, Colonel. Come on then, Carleton. Let's not keep the Colonel waiting too long."

While the Colonel ordered another Ramos Gin Fizz, Jannings and Inslee returned to their rooms. Jannings showered and put on a suit and tie and a straw boater. He met Inslee in the lobby, also in suit and tie, but wearing a black derby.

"I must say, Jay, this sure is interesting."

"Oh, the Colonel's a character. That is a fact."

The Packard awaited them at the foot of the staircase. They got inside the rear compartment and, facing backward, sat opposite Thatcher on plush upholstery. It was a short drive down US 1 to Target City. The Packard cruised past the tourist camp crammed full of tents and trailers, and the dog track, empty until night came.

"Since you boys were nice enough to keep me company, I should do you a good turn back. How much money do you have on you?"

Jannings laughed. "What? Do you mean *cash* money?"

"Yes, exactly. The old elusive spondulix, as it's sometimes known."

"I guess about a hundred."

"And I've got fifty," Inslee said. "But, Colonel, what are you—?"

"Never mind that, Jayson. Just hand over the money. I'll give it back shortly."

Puzzled, they nonetheless took out their wallets and handed the bills to Thatcher. He placed them in his old-fashioned long wallet and slipped it into a coat pocket. The chauffeur turned the car onto Prosperity Causeway. They soon reached Target City, a booming resort town on a narrow peninsula with a deepwater bay. Rather than head to Spanish Square, the center of town, they turned left on Ocean Drive, the main drag, and right again on North 1st Street. The chauffeur parked the car beside a one-story whitewashed stucco building with a flat roof. It was partly concealed by tall palms and other heavy tropical foliage.

They walked down a winding flagstone path. A small, painted tin sign beside the door read Orange Blossom Land & Investment Company. Thatcher deftly pressed the buzzer with his cane. A large black man in a dark suit opened the first door. He grinned.

"Hello, Moze," Thatcher said.

"How do, Colonel. Mr. Easton's expecting you. Hold on while I let y'all in."

A loud buzzer sounded and an iron-barred screen door popped open. Thatcher pulled it wide and gestured in a courtly manner for Jannings and Inslee to go first. They entered a large room filled with tobacco smoke. Men sat in easy chairs; their expensive clothes and shoes and the fine cigars they smoked showed their obvious wealth. They ignored the newcomers, but instead conversed in low murmurs, their attention focused on a large blackboard mounted on a wall.

A tickertape machine ceaselessly clicked in a corner. Two men in shirtsleeves closely watched the tape, taking notes on pads. Frequently, one would go to the gridded blackboard, erase figures and chalk in new ones for companies like US Steel, General Electric, Westinghouse, and Sears. Some men smiled when the figures changed while others ruefully frowned.

Moze returned. "Mr. Easton will see you gentlemen now. This way, please."

They went through a back door into a luxuriously furnished office with a white leather couch. Another tickertape machine chattered away in a corner. Paintings filled the walls with seascapes and portraits. Three black telephones stood in a neat row on the mahogany desk. Rising to greet them was a man in a white suit and black tie. He was big, with broad shoulders. His thick black hair was combed back with a light brilliantine sheen.

The man's mustache, trimmed to a thin, continuous straight line, straightened further with his smile. "Colonel. Good to see you. I see you brought some folks along."

"Harry. Come here, you young devil."

They wrung hands and slapped each other's backs. Thatcher introduced Easton to Inslee and Jannings, smiling broadly as they shook hands.

"Nice to meet you fellows. Are you in business with the Colonel?"

"No, I thought the boys might find the office interesting. Carleton is thinking about becoming a broker."

"Well, this is a good place to learn. We make as much down here as they do on Wall Street and without the bad weather and traffic. I tell you what, why not sit in the main office awhile? You'll get an idea of how things run. It's not that different from anywhere else."

"You can pass time while Harry and I discuss business."

Easton pressed a buzzer. The door opened. "Moze. Find chairs for these gentlemen. See that they're comfortable."

"Yes, sir. This way, gentlemen," Moze said, leading Inslee and Jannings to armchairs near the cashier's booth. He fetched iced lemonade and provided cigars. They puffed cigars, sipped lemonade, and watched the board.

One stock drew particular attention: Ryan Tire Company. After reaching a peak of forty seven dollars per share, the price tumbled dramatically to thirty eight, then twenty nine, then seventeen. Plainly angry and miserable, men tore up their vouchers and left. One man went to the cashier and laid his vouchers on the counter.

"I'd like to redeem these put warrants, please."

The clerk whistled. "That's the fifth stock you've shorted this week, Mr. Blassic. You got a crystal ball?"

"Just hard work and study, John."

"Shall I send a deposit draft to Square Deal Bank?"

"I'll take my returns here. I want to invest in land right away."

Jannings and Inslee watched as twelve individual thousand-dollar bills were laid on the marble countertop. The man casually took the money, slipped it into a coat pocket, and left.

"They play for big stakes," Jannings whispered.

"You ain't just whistling Dixie."

Thatcher showed up shortly afterward. He redeemed a voucher with the cashier and then turned to them, all grinning affability. "Let me take you back to the hotel. We can have dinner together. My treat, of course."

"Now, Colonel, let us pay our share. You're being too generous."

"Nonsense, Jayson. Come. The car's waiting." Once inside the car, Thatcher said, "I said I'd make it worth your while." He pulled out his wallet and handed four hundred dollars to Jannings and two hundred to Inslee. Jannings stared at the crisp money in his open palm.

"That's your share of the returns from Ryan Air. It's not much but should cover your hotel bill."

"You mean it will pay for tonight's dinner, Colonel."

"No, no. I said dinner is my treat. But, since you insist, Jayson, you can buy the second bottle of champagne."

At the hotel, they dined in a private room on foie gras, caviar, pheasant under glass, grilled steaks and chops, washed down with French champagne smuggled from Cuba for a king's ransom.

Expansive under alcohol's influence, Thatcher held forth about another deal. "There's a two-bit company in New Jersey. Weehawken Electric. The shares don't trade much over five apiece. What people don't know is the company has perfected a fluorescent lamp that runs for years. When the patent's registered and news gets around, the company's stock will soar."

"How do you know this, Colonel?" Jannings asked.

"Why, I found a clerk who works for the company. Got him good and drunk. Bribed him. How else do you think business gets done? I want you boys in on the ground floor with me. Are you game?"

"Of course, I'm game. Up to the hilt."

"Good man, Carleton. What about you, Jayson? Are you up for a flutter?"

"Certainly, Colonel, although I don't know if I can really contribute anything significant."

"Every bit helps. Now, I plan to invest a hundred thousand of my own money. What do you boys propose to put in?"

Jannings thought briefly. "I could get a wire from my trust fund for twenty thousand dollars."

"A nice round sum. And you, Jayson?"

"Father keeps me on a tight leash. I could get maybe two thousand."

"A more than acceptable amount. Now we have a few days before the news gets out, ample time if we move fast, boys. And now for more champagne."

* * * * *

It took two days and several telegrams before Jannings's trustee consented to wire the money from his trust fund to the Square Deal Bank, located in the Target City Tower in Spanish Square, the very day Weehawken Electric would announce its new patent. The cashier counted the money out in neat piles of hundreds, wrapped them tight with rubber bands, and slipped them into a large manila envelope.

Inslee awaited him outside. "Let's catch the streetcar and go to the office. We need to be quick."

Streetcars ran the length of Ocean Drive. Inslee and Jannings boarded a northbound one. "Will the Colonel meet us at the office?"

Inslee shook his head. "He was called away on business at the last moment, but you needn't worry. The Colonel provided specific instructions along with a power of attorney to act on his behalf. Look. He also gave me this."

Inslee showed Jannings a certified check for one hundred thousand dollars drawn on the First Bank of Savannah. "We'll hand this over with our money to Easton and tell him to invest it in Weehawken Electric. Only we buy the stock on margin, ten percent down on each share. That way we get ten times as much stock for our investment."

Jannings frowned. "Won't we have to pay the other ninety percent?"

"Sure, but not right away. And when it comes due, we can *easily* pay for it out of profits. The patent will be announced after noon. The stock will take off. All we have to do then is decide when to sell and cash in our earnings."

Inslee rubbed his hands in anticipation. Jannings grinned so much his face started to hurt. They got off at North 1st Street and walked to the office. As before, Moze greeted them with a broad smile and led them to Easton, on the phone.

"OK, J.L...Yes...I'll put you down for fifty thousand shares of Consolidated Copper...And I'll unload them as soon as the quarterly earnings reports come out...Don't worry. The deal will go...J.L., the deal will go down exactly the way you want it...Okay...Yes, sir...So long." Easton hooked the phone and smiled. "Hello, fellows. What can I do for you today?"

Inslee took out the cashier's check and set it on the desk. "We'd like to make an investment. On behalf of ourselves and the Colonel."

Easton's eyes went wide. He whistled softly. "The Colonel's hunting big game again."

"And we have our own contribution to make." Jannings set down his money. Inslee added his. Easton carefully counted and noted the amounts beside their names in a ledger.

"So what do you want this money invested in? With this large an amount, you ought to diversify, put it in a mix of investments."

"We want to buy shares of Weehawken Electric on margin, ten percent down on each share."

Easton studied them, dark eyes alive with curiosity. "Weehawken Electric? That's not what you'd call a high return for your money. Shares are lucky to go much over seven."

"Nevertheless, that's what we want to buy, Mr. Easton," Jannings said.

"OK. I'm only the broker. The Colonel probably knows something I don't. Let me get a quote and I'll put you down for a hundred and twenty two thousand dollars worth of Weehawken Electric common shares on ten percent margin."

Easton spoke briefly over another phone, did calculations on a Burroughs Adding Machine and wrote down several figures in pencil. He turned his pad around and showed them the numbers.

"I can give you two hundred and fifty five thousand shares at five and three-quarters per with a margin call if the price drops anywhere under two. Is that agreeable? Jayson? Carleton?"

They both eagerly nodded.

"Then sign here."

The deal done, they sat with their share vouchers in the main office. As before, Moze brought them lemonade and cigars. Weehawken Electric was listed near the bottom of the board. The price stayed at five and three-quarters but edged up to six at eleven-thirty. Inslee nudged

Jannings. "Someone else must have found out. Watch it rocket after twelve."

The pair watched as seconds slowly squeezed past and the clock hand moved toward twelve. Inslee sat with teeth clenched. He continually turned the brim of his derby around in his hands. The appointed time came and went. By two o'clock the price was still at six.

"Do you think something went wrong?" Jannings whispered to Inslee.

"I don't know. It's supposed to start going up. Wait, here comes a board-marker. This is probably it."

The board marker erased the figure for Weehawken Electric. Instead of an increase, he chalked in four.

Inslee almost bolted from his chair. He shouted, "What? That's not supposed to happen."

"Quiet, Jay. People can hear you."

Shortly after the price was marked to three and a quarter, and then three. Lemonade and cigars forgotten, Jannings and Inslee watched glumly as the board-marker went to the board and marked Weehawken Electric down to two and a half. Inslee grabbed Jannings hard by the wrist.

"What are we going to do? We'll be ruined."

"Get a hold of yourself, Jay. Wait and see if the price recovers."

The board-marker chalked in one and a half. No one noticed in the busy, noisy office, but Inslee and Jannings slumped in their chairs like men under a death sentence. Moze came up and spoke in a discreet, low tone.

"Gentlemen. Mr. Easton would like to see you."

Easton sat behind his desk, dead serious. He didn't smile. He didn't ask them to sit down. He regretfully shook his head. "I told you not to put all your eggs in one basket, but you insisted. Now it's your funeral. Whatever you thought was going to happen with Weehawken Electric, it's falling like an anvil, well below two dollars a share. Do you know what that means?"

"We lose the money we put up?" Jannings said.

Easton nodded. "That, and both of you and the Colonel are also on the hook for over a million dollars more in liability for the margin call. There's no way around it, boys. That money has to be paid."

Inslee complained. "Look. You don't understand. It wasn't supposed to happen this way. The Colonel had inside information. There's a patent for a fluorescent—"

Easton silenced Inslee with an upraised palm. "Even a sharp operator like the Colonel gets a bum steer now and then, Mister Inslee. And it doesn't change the fact that the margin must be paid. Now."

Jannings placed his palms on the desk and shook his head. "Mr. Easton, you don't understand. My family has *some* money, but most of it is tied up in property and other investments. I can't cover a sum like that. The Colonel said this was a sure-fire thing. Isn't there something you can do for us?"

For a long, painful interval, Easton appraised them, coolly, silently, fingers steepled over his chest. He suddenly pointed to the couch.

"Have a seat."

They sat.

Easton smiled reassuringly. "Boys, I understand this is your first time playing the market. You didn't expect to get in a jam. I also understand you simply followed the Colonel's instructions. He'll have to make this margin good. He has deep pockets and you don't."

"That's right. The Colonel's the man you need to speak to," Inslee said.

"So what I propose is this. I'll look to the Colonel as the primary source to pay the margin call and leave you out of the matter. The only way

I'll have recourse against you is if things don't work out with him. And I know that won't happen since he's an old-fashioned gentleman and a man of his word."

"So we don't have to pay the margin?"

"That's right, Carleton. I'm holding you harmless."

"Can we get our money back?"

Easton frowned and spoke sharpish. "Don't push your luck, Mister Inslee. I'm doing you both a big favor. Just be glad you're getting off with a light haircut and not a total scalping. Now if you don't mind, I've got to get back to work."

He pressed the buzzer. Moze opened the door and graciously gestured for them to leave. Inslee was about to protest some more, but Jannings grabbed him by a sleeve and yanked him out.

"This isn't right. I lost two thousand dollars—" Inslee whined.

"And I've lost twenty. Come on. Don't make a fool of yourself."

They took a taxi to the hotel. Jannings stared out the window, unable to register anything, focused on his loss. Inslee railed against Thatcher.

"All the time he proclaimed himself the slickest item in Dixie, the surefire stock picker, and he hands us a dog like this. Carleton, I apologize for introducing you to that man. If I had any idea he'd make us lose the shirts off our backs, I'd have shot him down like a dog instead."

"Calm down, Jay. We should give the Colonel a chance to explain himself."

"I plan to do just that. I'm checking out and driving straight back to Savannah. I can probably make it in twenty four hours."

Inslee was true to his word. Tight-faced with rage, he jammed his clothes into two suitcases. Jannings carried one downstairs for him. Inslee paid his bill. Outside, a valet brought up his car, a small, low-slung '23 Alfa Romeo. The valet put the luggage in the car.

"I won't even say hello to my folks first. I'll look up Thatcher and make him pay back our money or learn the reason why he won't."

"Will you stay in touch with me, Jay?"

"I already thought of that." Inslee handed Jannings a slip of paper. "That's my family address. Write me there. Give me your address so I can send you the money. Here's a pencil."

Jannings scribbled his address on another paper scrap and handed it to Inslee. They shook hands. Inslee got into the running car and left. Jannings waved goodbye to his friend.

* * * * *

For the rest of his stay at the Sanford Hotel, Jannings checked the front desk every morning for a message. Only, his box remained empty. Worried about running into Easton, he avoided Target City, even declined an invitation from a cute flapper to go dancing at a new club, a headache as his poor excuse. When he returned to his family home in Orange, Connecticut, he wrote to Inslee in Savannah only to have his letter returned, marked "Return To Sender. No Such Address." He sat in his bedroom, at his desk, the returned letter in one hand. Dim recognition slowly stole over him.

"I've been cheated."

* * * * *

They sat in Easton's office drinking gin and tonics with plenty of fresh lime juice the way Easton liked them. He totaled figures on a pad.

"So we cut up the score like this. Hiram gets eleven thousand, out of which I take a two thousand dollar cut. Eleven hundred split to Moze and the shills, and five hundred goes to the fix."

"It all sounds in order, Harry." Hiram Pigus, the Kentucky Colonel, idly fanned himself with his broad-brimmed straw hat.

"Correct. That leaves nine thousand for Eddie with you paying the cap from your cut."

"That's jake with me," said Eddie Mines, the Mormon Kid.

Easton sipped his drink. "It was a nice touch, Hiram. You worked the rag on Jannings like silk. Eddie roped him and you hooked him like a fish."

"We had him cold when he saw John lay those coarse ones out on the counter," Mines said. "That pile of thousands turns the trick every time."

"Still, we should have left Jannings on the hook for awhile longer, see if he was good for another touch. Try to work a long con on him."

Pigus laughed. "Harry, I'm too old to work long cons. Especially with boring Yankee sprigs like that."

"Amen there, Hiram. And I'm too young to waste time."

Harry shook his head. "That's where you're both wrong. You should always be trying to work a bigger, longer con. That's what really pays."

"Whatever you say, Harry. You're the boss. How about another drink?"

"Sure, kid, sure."

Mark Mellon is a novelist who supports his family by working as an attorney. He has four novels and seventy short stories (many as reprints) published in the USA, UK, Ireland, and Denmark.

Short fiction by Mark has been recently published in the magazines Thriller and Tigershark, and Lovecraftiana. His novella *Escape From Byzantium* won the 2010 Independent Publisher Silver Prize for SF/Fantasy.

This story is excerpted from the 40,000-word unpublished novella *The Bigger Con*.

mellonwritesagain.com

Paul & Three Pistols

Lee Blevins

Paul sat on the stool behind the counter, reading a comic book as he often did at work, when the screen door swung open and a girl in a summer dress and a pair of punk boots shuffled inside. She looked at Paul. Her reddish bangs, cut short but sharp, dipped. He nodded back.

"Morning," he said.

"It's afternoon."

Paul was about to say something, anything really, when there entered a man who could have been a cross between a cowboy and a 1950s greaser or, more likely, a film student at a costume party. The man glanced at Paul with just a hint of sharpness. The screen door slapped shut behind him. Then he followed the girl as she slid down the nearest aisle.

Paul watched them for a moment. Her dress flowing in the breeze the screen door enabled. His back pockets taut beneath the hem of his denim jacket. Their boots softer than one might have supposed. Then he decisively looked away.

In the top corner of his eyes, which couldn't help but catch their half-formed figures at the edges of his vision, he saw her kneel down in front of the two long boxes that lay beneath the Little Debbie snack stand.

She flipped through the old comics.

"Overrated," she said, turning each floppy like an oversized playing card, "trash . . . mediocre . . . halfway decent."

Paul looked up but couldn't see what she had chosen. She glanced at the man in denim.

"Get it," he told her.

She pulled one comic away from the rest.

Paul looked down at his comic again. He heard them continue toward the back wall. There came the refrigerated whisk of a cooler door opening.

"More of this shit?" the man said.

"When in Kentucky..." the girl replied.

A tinkling of glass and then the door was shut again. Looking up, Paul saw them turn from the Ale-8 cooler to swerve down the bread aisle.

He was suddenly worried that if they picked up a box of macaroni and cheese it would be dusty underneath. Not might be but would be. That was the kind of establishment he helped run.

As they neared, and without pausing at its place on the shelf, the man in denim said, "I'm never gonna eat a can of Vienna weenies again."

"I don't mind them much."

They came to the counter. Paul placed his comic book to the side, still opened, near the landline phone, and got up from the stool. He smiled.

"Find everything you need?"

First the man and then the girl sat their Ale-8s on the counter. The man had grabbed a bag of chocolate-covered donuts. The girl placed her comic book beside it. It was Dreadstar, of all things.

"Could we use your restroom?" she asked.

"Sure." Paul pointed down the length of the deli counter, where turkey and ham and cheese and lettuce and tomato, beneath rounded glass, waited to be sliced. The door in the far corner was marked Bathroom. "We just have the one."

"Dibs," the girl said.

She went.

The man in denim turned, making only fleeting eye contact with Paul, and ran his gaze over the cigarettes stuffed into their tiny cubbies along the wall. His mouth pinched as if he was chewing an invisible toothpick. Then loosened.

"I want a carton of Marlboro Lights," he said.

"Can do."

Paul approached the cigarette wall, pulled out a carton, and turned back to the counter. The man was old enough, but he knew he should double check ID anyway; somehow he couldn't bring himself to do it. The man in denim glanced at the sign with the poorly drawn pig tacked above the food prep table behind the deli display. "Do you have pulled pork or is it more like a sloppy joe?"

"It's a little sloppy," Paul admitted.

The man in denim locked sardonic eyes on Paul. "How about your hot dogs? Are they fake, too?"

"No, they're good. Especially with the sauce." It was his mother's recipe, but good was perhaps an overstatement.

The man nodded. "I'll try one."

Paul moved to get the man a hot dog as the girl in the summer dress came out of the bathroom. He put a cardboard container down and unrolled the bag of buns.

"Swap you," said the man to the girl.

On the far side of the deli glass, in his peripheral vision, Paul watched the man's stride, all sharp hips and coiled manhood. He reached for a set of tongs.

"This place is dry, right?" the girl asked from behind.

"The county is." Paul placed the dog in the bun and closed the lid. "But the city isn't."

"What city?"

Paul flipped up the top of the sauce pot next. Steam coated its underside.

"You had to have passed through it, right? Clearland?"

"I was just being a snob," the girl said. Paul picked up the ladle for the sauce and dipped it inside. She asked him, "How long have you worked here, mister?"

"Seven years." It took him half that long to get good enough at preparing hot dogs to stop spilling sauce off the bun. He placed the ladle in the sink and closed the sauce pot. When he glanced back at the girl, he was a tad unnerved to find her staring straight at him.

"Does he like mustard and ketchup?" Paul asked.

"Give him everything," she said.

Paul carried the hot dog, fully garnished, to the counter. He sat its cardboard container down beside the twin Ale-8s. The girl pointed one beringed finger at the comic book Paul had left beside the telephone. She raised her eyebrows.

They were almost thick, and darker than the shade of her hair.

"You didn't get Saga here," she said.

"No, we only sell back issues. I got that at the comic bookstore in town."

"They have comic bookstores in Clearland?" It was as if he had told her that the county didn't have a higher cancer rate than most of the rest of the country.

"Just one," he said. "The back issues we do have. I mean, no one buys them. Except this one kid down the creek. But my uncle likes them there. He's Halsey."

Her face went blank but her eyes didn't. "Who's Halsey?"

"This is his hutch."

"What's a hutch?"

Paul pointed to the faded sign above his head. It showed a sketched replica of the store they were in with the words Halsey's Hutch beneath it.

"The place is named after him."

The man in denim stepped out of the bathroom and strode over to the girl.

"This is a hutch," she told him. "It's named after his uncle."

The man looked first at the hot dog and then at the girl. He said, "I thought a hutch was something a rabbit hid in."

She shrugged. "Maybe he should have."

The man reached his right hand below the counter and when he raised it again he was holding a handgun. He aimed that at Paul.

The man's tone was casual, almost routine. "I know you probably don't make much here but give us all you do."

Paul breathed. He remembered how. He nodded — twice — and then he managed to get the cash register open.

The girl sounded less bored. "This store is so old and cheap I don't think we gotta worry about any hidden alarms, babe."

"Yeah," said the man with the gun. "I bet they've got a telegraph back there somewhere."

Paul stared down at how pitiful the cash drawer was. He laid the few bills beside all the other stuff the couple wasn't going to pay for.

"We only want quarters," she said. "None of the rest of the change."

"Unless it's already rolled," the man amended.

"Yeah, unless it's rolled."

Paul dropped a handful of quarters beside the cash. He retrieved one that slipped through his fingers. Then he added a thin roll of pennies. The man in denim tapped the barrel of the pistol against the top of the cash register, near the analog display.

"Raise up underneath," he said. "Where you keep the checks. People still write checks here, don't they? Or are you still operating under a store credit system?"

"Yeah," said Paul, too scared to be offended.

He pressed his fingers against the latches on the side of the cash drawer and slid it up and out. He rested the drawer on the edge of the counter.

There were several checks, a couple of credit card receipts, and a dozen EBT slips beneath it.

"Shuffle that around."

Paul looked up at the gun. "What?" he said, too sharp. "I don't—"

The man was patient, at least then. "We got to make sure there's no more cash in there."

"Oh." Paul reached in and carefully, yet shakily, ran his fingers through the paper slips. They didn't have a secret stash. Just dust and one button for some reason.

He made eye contact.

"Are there bags under the counter?" the man asked him.

Paul nodded.

"Is there a gun down there?"

Paul shook his head no.

"Get us a bag," said the man in denim. "Brown if you got it."

"That's all we do have."

The girl in the summer dress smiled. "They're environmentalists, honey. We need to check our preconceived notions."

Paul bent down beneath the level of the counter. The edge of the tile gave way to plywood paneling and then to the darkness of a shelf inset. They stacked the brown bags in two sections.

He couldn't see the gun anymore and he wasn't sure if the man with the gun could see him but he knew all it would take is one lean forward and then brains out, Paul Halsey.

He grabbed the top brown bag from the right stack and rose again on cracking knees. He shook the bag open with the practiced jerk of a store clerk. Then he stood the bag on the counter.

"Should I?"

The girl nodded. "Full service, mister."

It wasn't much, of course. Just two Ale-8s, a bag of donuts, and a carton of cigarettes. He put every-thing into the brown bag except the hot dog and the comic book.

"Do you want to carry that?" he asked her, referring to the comic book.

She nodded. "I'll take yours, too."

Paul almost sighed. Then he picked up Saga and laid it atop Dreadstar. Both space operas, he realized, after a fashion. The girl in the summer dress scooped up both comics, as well as the brown paper bag. The Ale-8s inside clinked together. Still aiming, the man in denim grabbed the hot dog and took a big bite. He chewed it with an expression that revealed neither way whether he liked what he tasted. His mouth shifted like a waterbed. The barrel of the pistol was small and dark and full of terrible promise. His lips grew still.

Then he blew his half-chewed food out in one gigantic spit that sounded like a wet gunshot. Hot dog particles slammed into Paul's face. Bits of food dripped down his cheeks, warm and putrid out of context. The girl laughed. It was short and savage and somehow it hurt Paul more than the shock did. He wasn't brave enough to wipe the shit away.

The man in denim grinned. "You're lucky that's not your brains."

Then he and the girl turned and walked out. The screen door tap-tap-tapped behind them.

Paul wiped his face clear with one slick hand motion. He heard a car engine kick in outside and rose up at the window on his tiptoes. His view was half-obscured by the open sign. A red car with Virginia plates darted across the parking lot, came to a slammed halt beside the road, waited impatiently for a white van to pass, and then swung out onto the highway. They picked up speed at a maniacal rate. In three seconds and one turn, they were gone.

Paul breathed deeper. He wiped off more food. Looked down at the floor. There was a lot to clean up but less than there might have been. Of course, he wouldn't have been the one cleaning that up. At that morbid thought, his knees buckled and he found himself curling into a crouch.

He steadied his weight against the metal side of the display counter. His stomach swirled. Paul grabbed the nearest stack of brown bags and yanked them out so hard the stack itself swayed before it fell onto the floor. He had caught one, though, and he opened it with both hands.

He stared at the pistol Uncle Clyde kept below the counter, hidden behind the paper bags, the one he had been too afraid to reach for, and then he dry-heaved into the warm dark of the bag.

* * * * *

Paul washed his hands before he dialed 911. (They smelled of hot dog sauce.) It rang twice before the dispatcher answered.

"Beckham County 911."

"I've just been robbed," Paul said. "At gunpoint."

The dispatcher took this information with a minimum of excitement. "Is the robber still there?"

"Robbers. And no, they left."

"Where are you?" She sounded like she spent a lot of her time at the library, either behind the desk or checking out romance novels. "Where did this happen?"

"Halsey's Hutch." Paul had to think twice for the address. "7830 U.S. 60 East. I work here."

"Do you know which direction they went when they left?"

"Towards Carter County." Paul realized the series of low clicks he heard was the dispatcher's speed typing.

"What were they driving?" she asked him.

"A red car."

"What kind of red car?"

"I'm sorry," said Paul. "I'm really bad at cars."

"Did you happen to catch their license plate?"

Paul looked down at his grass-stained sneakers, which rested on the wooden bar that ran around the middle of the stool. "I'm bad at license plates, too."

"That's okay." But she wasn't so professional she made it sound like it. "What's your name?"

"Paul Halsey. H-a-l-s-e-y."

"What did they look like, Paul? The people who robbed you?"

"It was a man and a woman. A couple. Youngish. White." He tried to recall their faces. Succeeded. Especially hers. "Good looking."

"What were they wearing?"

Paul scratched at the side of his neck. He found some mustard smeared there. "He was all in denim. She had a dress with some pattern on it. Flowers or trees."

"You said they had guns?"

"He had a gun. A handgun." Or was it a pistol? How should he put it, technically speaking?

"Okay, Paul. A police officer will be by shortly."

Paul checked the clock mounted beside the television on the wall. "How long do you think is shortly?"

"I can't be sure. But the robbers aren't currently in the area, correct?"

He checked out the window. "Not currently."

"Then," said the dispatcher, with a practiced chill, "we'll have someone out to see you as soon as possible."

He knew that was the best he was going to get so he told her, "Okay." Even added, "Thank you."

"No, thank you, Mr. Halsey." The dispatcher hung up. Paul didn't have time to obsess over just how passive-aggressive the last thing she said might have been. He set the phone in its cradle.

But didn't let go.

He raised the phone again and placed its Siamese ends against the side of his face. Paul pressed a series of numbers he knew by heart. Waited until he heard the click.

"You better come over, Clyde. We just got robbed."

* * * * *

Carrying a shotgun, Clyde Halsey burst into the store he had named after himself. He was wearing a tie-dye shirt over a pair of camo shorts. His gray Willie Wonka hair looked almost windswept. He was out of breath because he had walked at a fairly quick pace for nearly one hundred yards from his house all the way to the store. He was sixty two, overweight, and lazy by well-earned inclination.

"Did they hurt you?" he asked.

Paul's left index finger swirled around the air in the general direction of the shotgun. "You can't have that here."

Clyde hefted the shotgun up, his more wrinkled index finger not that close to the trigger. "The hell I can't."

The old man went past the end of the deli counter and turned to come behind it. His garish yellow Crocs slapped at the tile in approach.

"Seriously," said Paul. "The police are on their way. That's gonna make them nervous."

Clyde stopped between the food prep counter and the deli display case. He shrugged. "This is America. They're already nervous."

Then, in a complete violation of sanitation norms, he placed his shotgun on the counter so that the barrel was beneath the hot dogs and the stock was under their sauce.

"How much did they get?" Clyde asked him.

"Like, thirty dollars."

"That's sort of sad, ain't it?" Clyde shook his head. Paul admitted it was…a little. "Anyone we know?"

"No. Strangers. A guy and a girl."

"What? Both of them?"

Paul nodded.

"They both had guns?"

"No, only he had a gun. "

"She was an active participant?"

Paul smiled. "You find that so hard to believe? It's 2018, Clyde. There were bad girls in Bible days."

"Hey," said Clyde, heading toward the back, "I'm just glad you didn't get shot." He picked up the folded lawn chair that leaned against the wall. "And that we didn't make more money today."

Clyde opened the lawn chair and placed it at an angle so that he could easily look at both Paul and the television, whichever needed his attention more in the moment. Before he sat down himself, he crossed the floor to the cigarette display and snatched a pack of Kentucky's Best from it.

"Come on," said Paul. "You've been doing so good."

Clyde was already tearing the cellophane from around the cardboard. "Let something halfway pleasant come out of this matter," he said.

He dumped the cellophane onto the floor. His uncle wouldn't be the one to sweep it up later. Clyde packed the cigarettes, flipped open the lid, and pulled one out. He slid the pack into his camo pocket, retrieved a lighter he had stuffed in there for the other substance he sometimes smoked, and lit the cigarette. It wasn't technically legal to smoke inside a place of business within Beckham County limits, but Clyde didn't let that stop him any more than his heart attack had.

"I'm sorry," said Paul.

"What for?"

"I let them take it. I didn't even think about it. Our pistol."

Clyde's second inhale in six months rapidly followed his first. "That probably would have been a mistake."

"You would've done it."

The old man left his cigarette dangling in the corner of his mouth like he used to. "Not for thirty dollars," he said.

"And two comic books."

That got Clyde to pull the cigarette out. "You're kidding?"

"Nope."

"He was a geek?"

"She was…something."

"A woman thief?" Clyde said. "I'll buy it. A girl who likes comic books? Sure. But a woman thief who likes comic books? That's some *Pulp Fiction* bullshit." He ashed on the floor. Glanced down. He wasn't looking at the cellophane. "Why are there little bits of hot dog on the floor?"

* * * * *

The cruiser slid into the parking lot, lights on and siren off. The state trooper parked to the side of the screen door, past the ice machine. Paul could clearly see his cruiser through the window.

The trooper stepped out with his hat on his head and an expensive-looking clipboard in hand. It reminded Paul of Robert Patrick in *Terminator 2: Judgment Day* when the trooper turned his head to make eye contact through the window.

"He's here," Paul whispered to Clyde. "Try to behave now."

Seconds later the hinges of the screen door squeaked as the state trooper pulled it open. He didn't step inside just yet.

"They're not still around, are they?" He had a soft Southern accent that wasn't quite local.

"No, sir," said Paul.

The trooper stepped inside. He didn't let gravity shut the screen door, he eased it closed himself. *Woods* was embroidered on his uniform shirt, above his shiny badge. He looked between Paul, on the stool, and Clyde, who sat in the chair in the back with his head just above the counter like some kind of haunted hippie ghost.

"Who's who?" asked Woods.

"He works here," said Clyde. "I own here."

"Both of you were here?"

"Just me," said Paul.

Woods stepped all the way up to the counter. He spotted the shotgun and shifted his right hand back an inch nearer his holster.

"What's with the firearm?"

Paul looked at Clyde. "I told you. What did I tell you?"

"That's for if they come back," his uncle explained.

"I don't like it," said Woods. "How do I know you're who you say you are?"

Clyde got up from the chair and took a swing of a step around. "The name on the sign is Halsey's Hutch. We're Halseys. I'm Clyde. He's Paul."

Woods' hard eyes panned up to the sign above their heads and then down again. "Show me your IDs."

"Sir," Clyde said, polite enough, "I don't have to show you shit."

"Clyde…"

The trooper looked at Paul with an irritated misery that was in search of company. "What is he, a sovereign citizen or something?"

Paul turned on his uncle. "Show him your goddamn license, please."

"There's such a thing as the Second Amendment." Clyde went to the counter. He reached for his back pocket. "I'm getting my wallet. Try not to shoot me."

"Come on, man," said Woods.

Paul pulled his wallet first. He laid it down on the counter, open so that his driver's license looked out from its plastic sleeve. Clyde followed suit. His wallet had a pot leaf sticker on it.

The trooper stepped closer and examined both IDs. Nodded. Then stepped back. "That didn't have to be so goddamn difficult," he said. Then, to Paul, "Tell me about the reason you called."

"About an hour ago…"

Clyde cut in. "Thank God it wasn't no emergency. He would've been dead by the time you decided to show up."

"…a man and a woman," continued Paul, "that I don't know, walk in here and they rob me."

Woods took notes with a pen he pulled out of his clipboard. "What did they look like?"

"Hipsters," said Paul. "White hipsters." The trooper gave him an expression he had previously reserved for Clyde. Paul tried again. "The man was wearing a Canadian tuxedo, the woman had on a dress."

"A Canadian what?" asked Woods.

"Tuxedo," said Paul. "Denim jacket, denim pants."

"You don't know what a Canadian tuxedo is?" asked Clyde. "Little kids in elementary school know that."

The trooper didn't reply. Paul noticed that he held his pen with only his thumb and his index finger. The middle finger was aloft as if it was a pretentious pinkie around a teacup handle. "Hair color?"

"She was, like, strawberry blonde. He was brown-haired, I guess. I'm not sure about him."

"Eye color?"

"I couldn't even begin to say."

"How tall were they?"

"He was about your height." Woods appeared about six-two. "She was a little shorter than me. I'm five-eight."

The trooper considered his next set of questions. "Did they mention each other's names? Or where they'd been, where they were going?"

"No," said Paul.

"What did they sound like? Were they from around here?"

"They didn't have much of an accent one way or the other."

"What were they driving?"

Paul sighed. He felt embarrassment oncoming.

"A red car."

"Make and model?"

"I don't know."

Woods had an efficient bedside manner. "Did you see a license plate?"

"No, I did not."

The trooper looked from Paul to Clyde, who had placed both hands on the counter like an annoyed pizzeria owner set to chew out some punks.

"Tell me you have a surveillance camera," Woods said.

"Never saw no need," replied Clyde.

"Well, I have and I just got here." The trooper turned to Paul. "How much did they take?"

"Thirty dollars and some change."

One more scribble. "Tell me how it happened."

Paul glanced at the window, then at the door, then at the state trooper. "They came in," he said. "Shopped a little. Used the bathroom. Then he put a gun in my face."

"What kind of gun?"

"A pistol." He managed not to leave a question mark on it.

"What kind of pistol?"

"He don't know pistols, neither," said Clyde.

"Let him answer."

"I don't know pistols, either."

This time the state trooper's nostrils flared. But just slightly. "And when they left, they drove toward the Carter County line?"

"Yeah."

"The sheriff's department over there is supposed to be on the lookout for suspicious red cars." Woods slid the pen into its clipboard holder. "Not much to go on."

Before his pride could prevent it, Paul said, "I'm sorry I can't help more."

Clyde offered that they were probably in Ashland by now, anyway.

"Why would you think they went to Ashland?" asked the trooper, with a hint of bitchiness.

With more than a hint of the same, Clyde said, "I don't think they went to Ashland. I just think you are late as all shit."

Paul cringed for him. But Woods seemed to take it in stride. He looked out the window. "I'm gonna go knock on some doors. See if anyone around here saw anything. Call in the description." Woods paused. "Vague as it is."

"Okay," said Paul.

The state trooper made eye contact with Paul. His eyes weren't cruel, but when they looked at you, you knew they were just businesslike. "I'll stop back in before I leave."

He went. Clyde stepped closer to the stool and they both watched through the window as Woods headed across the parking lot until he stepped out of sight. Then looked at each other.

"Jesus, Clyde," said Paul, "maybe you shouldn't act like a paranoid old hippie with thirteen pot plants in his basement."

"It's an even dozen."

* * * * *

Paul was washing his face in the sink when he looked over at the toilet and visualized her sitting there with her dress hiked up and a pair of panties, it didn't matter what color, stretched between her knees. He could almost hear the stream.

And then he imagined the man in denim standing there with his big angry cock in one hand and his little calm pistol in the other. That sounded more like thunder. Paul turned off the faucet. He pulled a paper towel out of the dispenser and wiped his face dry. He tossed the towel into the trash can before he left the bathroom. Woods was back. He stood not talking with Clyde. Paul headed down the customer side of the deli counter. The trooper looked at him.

"Did anyone see anything?" Paul asked.

Woods checked a note on his clipboard. "Nina Marsh saw their car leave. She didn't get the license plate, either, but she said it was some kind of Chevy."

"That's something."

"Wouldn't be much, actually. Not usually. But I just heard from dispatch that a gas station got robbed in Louisa three hours ago. A man and a woman. And that they got on camera."

"You think it was the same people?"

Woods didn't need to check the clipboard. He had this information fresh in his head. "2009 Chevrolet Malibu. Red. And the description matches."

Clyde held both his arms out at an angle as if he was cupping a big fat water balloon. "What did I tell you, Paul?" he asked. "This is some *Pulp Fiction* bullshit."

"What now?"

"Now we catch them," said Woods. "But, honestly, they're probably in Ohio already."

"Why do you think they went to Ohio?" Clyde just had to take a stab at revenge.

"I don't know, Mr. Halsey. Maybe they're driving around in goddamn circles." The trooper looked at Paul. "Your uncle gave me your number. I gave him my card. You should have one, too."

He opened his clipboard, it had a compartment inside, and he pulled out a business card. Paul took it. The card was dark and professional. Woods's first name was Roland.

"It's never easy," said Woods. "Someone pointing a gun at you. But you didn't get hurt, at least." Later, Paul would realize that his hesitation was the state trooper almost not telling him the next part. "They shot the gas station attendant."

"Is he okay?"

"No," said Woods. "He's dead."

All they could hear was a log truck barreling down U.S. 60.

Woods cleared his throat. "Call me, either of you, if you think of something. I'll do the same."

"Thank you — " Paul glanced at the card again. "Officer Woods."

"Trooper. We're called troopers."

"You've been a tremendous help, Trooper." The spin on it was Clyde's last little dig.

Woods looked over at him with two gun barrels where his eyes used to be. "You, too, Clyde."

Then he left. He didn't ease the screen door shut that time. Paul slid the business card into his breast pocket.

Clyde shook his head. "That is one rude cop."

* * * * *

That night, Paul parked his pickup truck in front of his trailer, which sat at the rear of a modest trailer park. He walked across the yard to the porch he and Clyde had added onto the trailer two years prior. Paul had a Batman welcome mat. He was a little too old to be embarrassed about it.

He unlocked the front door and let himself in. Max bounded up to him, the Corgi wagging what little tail he had, and applied a series of licks to his blue jeans.

"Hey, boy." Paul scratched Max behind the ears then walked to the island that separated the living room from the kitchen. He scooped up the leash. Its metal latch slapped against the side of the island as he turned.

Max was smart enough to be at the door already. Paul hooked the leash onto his collar and opened the screen door. This one, unlike the one at work, was glass. Max darted outside. Paul followed fast so the dog didn't get choked when he reached the end of his leash. They went down the steps and into the yard. Max didn't wait to find a perfect spot to pee. It had been several hours. Paul stared down the gravel road, bordered on either side by other trailer lots, his oh-so-wonderful neighbors, and toward the highway. He couldn't help but wonder what her name was.

* * * * *

He laid down to sleep about three beers and two cop show reruns later. He didn't know how long he laid there, in the dark, with Max curled above the covers between his ankles, warm but still awake. But he remembered his dream. In it, the man in denim was pointing the pistol at his face again, but closer this time.

And Paul, as if he wanted it that way, opened his mouth, took a step forward, and let the barrel of the pistol slide between his lips. While below the counter, balanced in a crouch, the girl in the summer dress made him gasp in surprise.

He woke up aroused.

Dawn was grayer than blue through the curtains. Paul grabbed the covers and fanned them upward until the snoring Max was lifted out of his spot and forced to drop onto the floor. Paul got up, boxer shorts tight, and stepped over to the bedroom door. Max looked at him in a halfway accusatory manner.

"Come on," said Paul, hating himself a bit. "Let's go for a walk."

That smoothed the problem over. Max darted out the door. He just didn't expect his owner to shut it behind him. As Paul got back in bed, Max caught on and started scratching at the bedroom door. Paul slid beneath the covers.

"I'm sorry, Max," he called out. "Now be quiet, will ya?"

Paul closed his eyes and began his fantasy by trying to picture her face. Finally managed to see it and her reddish bangs dipping as she knelt over him. "Good afternoon to you, too," he said to her, James Bond smooth.

* * * * *

Paul knew Clyde was in the store because the front door was open and the open sign was on. He parked his pickup in its customary spot, flush against the left side of the building. Got out. Clyde sat on the stool watching a western on TV. He hadn't bothered to sweep, mop, get anything ready for the deli, or do anything else for the store for that matter. He had basically just run up the electric bill. The only thing Clyde had lifted was the shotgun, which he left on the food prep table again.

"I thought I opened today," Paul said.

"And I thought you might want some company."

"Not if you don't put up that shotgun."

"This is my property," said Clyde. "All I'm doing is being prepared to defend myself."

"Can you at least not keep it next to the cutting board? The health inspector might not like it."

Clyde waved that concern away. "Sheila always tells me days before she does an inspection. That's small-town nepotism for you."

They had some big-town visitors later that day. A news crew, consisting of one reporter and one cameraman, pulled into the parking lot in a sleek van marked with sharp letters and a folded antenna system.

They recognized Valerie Spencer, of course. Anyone who watched WKYT would have. She was the go-to reporter for crime stories that happened outside of Lexington but still within the broadcast region. And she wanted to talk to them.

"I don't know," said Paul.

"Hold on a second," said Clyde, meeting the reporter in her almost overshadowed but still striking eyes. "That might be good for business."

"And we can get the word out on these criminals," said Valerie.

"That, too," Clyde added.

Valerie and Jerome, the cameraman, who bought four Airheads, one of each flavor they had plus an extra cherry, shot an introductory segment in the parking lot before they came inside to do the actual interview.

The reporter, holding a fuzzy microphone like a cute hammer, considered the counter with her arms crossed and the mic almost brushing her chin. "Do you think we could have you out of the shot for now, Clyde?"

"Sure," he said.

"And take that lawn chair with you."

Clyde picked it up, folded it, and stood there facing her like he had no place to call home anymore. "But where should I go?"

"Hmm." She gestured with her microphone. "With the turkey and ham?"

"Yeah," said Paul, "go join the rest of the meat."

"Watch it," said Clyde. Then he slunk off behind the deli counter, unfolded his chair, and sat down to watch Paul with the kind of resentment that only family members can feel.

"What do you think?" Valerie asked Jerome.

The cameraman had the camera on his shoulder and his right eye pressed into the viewfinder. He was as far back as one could get from the counter without being down an aisle.

"It works," he said.

"I can stand here?" Valerie was about a foot from the cash register.

"If we can get him to scoot his stool over."

Valerie looked at Paul with quite resourceful puppy dog eyes. For her, he would've scooted his stool for miles.

"Are we ready, Jerome?" He nodded.

Paul felt like he was already blushing, which he considered a particularly embarrassing possibility.

"Rolling."

Valerie flashed a smile and then she became Edward-Murrow serious. "What went through your mind when you saw that he had a gun?" she asked.

"I don't think I can say that on TV."

"How about when you realized you were being robbed? How did that feel?"

"Bad," said Paul. "Not good at all. Like a dangerous situation, you know."

Clyde would tease him for the rest of the day about how shitty an interview he gave but Paul found Clyde's answers embarrassing for different reasons. The old man actually told Valerie, "They're just glad I wasn't here," and then he revealed just where he had hidden his shotgun. Afterward, the news crew headed toward town to interview Trooper Woods.

"We'll be on at six," Valerie told them. Jerome went out the door. Valerie hesitated, then added, "You know, you really are lucky. Louisa was pretty tough."

And she left. Paul and Clyde wandered outside so they could watch them pack up the van. They waved as Jerome pulled out onto the highway.

"She's sexier on TV," Clyde said.

They only had two customers the rest of the day. The first was Ricky Sparks, all protein shake and almost-cleaned-off cow shit. He took a look around the place and told them, "I heard you got robbed."

"You heard right."

"Can I get some baloney?" he asked.

The second customer didn't leave so quick. It was Nina Marsh, with her infant daughter on her hip. She came for a loaf of bread, ostensibly, but really she just wanted to swap some information.

"I saw their car, you know."

"And you recognized its make and model?" Clyde barely hid his amusement.

Nina told them all about it. Then she made Paul tell her his side of the story. Clyde volunteered his. After he mentioned that he thought Trooper Woods was a bit of a dick, Nina defended him by saying that Roland was a very nice man with sexy thick neck muscles.

* * * * *

They closed the store three hours early so they could watch the broadcast from home. Paul's mother Mary drove over to her brother's house and cooked them all dinner. Clyde cleaned his kitchen stove just for the occasion. They ate in a dining room lined with bookshelves featuring a curious mix of Louis L'Amour and Terence McKenna, which was Clyde in bibliographic Venn diagram form. Mary lit a menthol cigarette after she took her last bite of mashed potatoes and held her burning cherry over her empty coffee cup.

"You should close that store, Clyde," she said, exhaling. "Ain't made money for fifteen years and it's getting dangerous."

"It isn't dangerous," he replied. "This is the first time it's ever been even slightly dangerous."

"Don't tell me it's not dangerous when someone just tried to kill my son."

"No one tried to kill me, Mom."

His mother gave Paul an expression with too much sass for it to come across as warm matronly wisdom. "Never point a gun at someone unless you're willing to pull the trigger. Your daddy taught you that." She turned back to her brother. "I just don't see the point in staying open anymore."

Paul thought about it. "Well," he said, "I'd rather have Clyde for a boss because he's family. And on assorted pain pills."

They settled down in the den shortly before six p.m., Clyde in his recliner and Mary and Paul on the loveseat. Clyde had a big-screen television, but it was one from the early '90s and it weighed about three hundred pounds. He bought it around the last time the store was profitable. Their news debut followed a commercial break about fifteen minutes through the broadcast. Valerie stood outside a

Marathon gas station that seemed not particularly busy. A graphic on the screen said she was in Louisa.

"Yesterday," she said, "at about one p.m., a man and a woman believed to be in the midst of a crime spree robbed this gas station and mortally wounded the attendant, one William Goggins, Jr."

The image cut to a close-up of an overweight but pretty woman with tears dried on her cheeks. Her name was Amanda Quisenberry, according to what the TV said, and below that they put the word Eyewitness.

"He did everything they asked him to," she told the camera. "No questions. But when they pushed me to the ground Mr. Goggins stuck up for me. And that's what they shot him for."

Now the TV showed an older woman sitting on a rocking chair on a front porch. She wasn't rocking and her posture was immaculate. Her name was Jenna Goggins. She was the widow.

"Lord make them pay for what they did to Willie. He was a good man and a great father and he helped rebuild our church. He didn't need to die for some drug money, or whatever they wanted it for."

The image cut to two still photographs, side-by-side, showing the man in denim and the girl in the summer dress. His was a mugshot, hers was a driver's license. Both their names were listed below their faces.

"Police say Joseph Canton and Ramey Mears, of Richmond, Virginia, are the suspects in the murder of William Goggins and at least one other armed robbery in Northeastern Kentucky. They should be considered armed and dangerous."

That's when it finally cut to Halsey's Hutch. Valerie addressed the camera from their parking lot. Paul realized why they had parked all the way beside the pine trees. It was so that their van wouldn't show up on-screen.

"Later that day," Valerie said, "Canton and Mears are also suspected to have robbed this convenience store situated ten miles outside of Clearland."

And there was Paul, looking more bloated and pale than he realized he was, with his name superimposed and everything.

"What went through your mind when you saw he had a gun?" Valerie asked him. Jerome had zoomed in so much that she was mostly offscreen.

They had edited the footage to make it flow better. On TV, he replied with an answer that in real life he didn't use yet, "Like a dangerous situation, you know."

Now Clyde was on-screen. He nodded, imperially. "They're just glad I wasn't here."

The broadcast switched to two flags, national and state, hanging limply in the breezeless sky outside the district post of the state police. "Hey," said Clyde, in the den, "they cut out the part where I showed them my shotgun."

Roland Woods even wore his hat at his desk. At least when doing TV interviews. His cubicle walls were the bland pop-up fabric of your average office job. The non-emergency contact number flashed. "Anyone with any information about their whereabouts should contact us. Help us catch them. Because they will get caught. Let it be as soon as they deserve."

The newscast went back to the newsroom. The anchor, who was handsome in a guidance counselor sort of way, thanked Valerie. She and Jerome had filmed Halsey's Hutch for over an hour for about thirty seconds of screen time.

Clyde told Mary, "That cop was pure asshole."

"I'm sure he liked you real well," she replied.

Paul turned down the volume and sat the remote down on the arm of the loveseat. His mother turned to him. "I didn't like the looks of the boy but the girl seemed pretty."

Paul nodded. "I thought so, too."

* * * * *

Paul first had the idea as he was driving home after dinner, but he laughed it off as crazy and planned not to revisit it. He failed. After he took Max for a walk, and on a whim, he decided to shut the dog out of the bedroom. Paul opened up Facebook on his laptop and typed her name into the search bar. There were three Ramey Mearses. She was the third. He could tell her from her thumbnail.

Max started scratching at the door. Paul had had to clean up flakes of paint and wood last time. Paul opened up her profile page. They had no friends in common. Her education listed was her high school and her most recent employer had been Dairy Queen.

He clicked on her profile picture to blow it up full-sized. Ramey Mears sat on a set of steps with her left hand cupping her chin and half a smile on her face. Paul tried to click around her pictures but her settings limited strangers and prevented that. So he just stared at that one picture for a while, eventually slipping his hand into his boxers. A short time later, he exited out of the full-screen picture and was about to exit out of the browser but didn't.

Instead, he moved the cursor back until it hovered over the send-a-friend-request button. He smiled at the absurdity of that thought. But stopped smiling the second a twitch, whether of nerves or of cruel fate, made him actually click on it. The request image shifted. He canceled it with another click. Paul slammed the laptop shut so fast he was lucky he didn't crack the screen.

* * * * *

Paul told himself she would never see it, and Ramey Mears wouldn't have ever seen it if she hadn't been on Facebook at the same moment that he sent it. She didn't recognize the name of the person who sent her the friend request but Facebook took her to his profile page when she clicked on it. Yeah, she recognized Paul's face. Joe, in the driver's seat, looked from the windshield which faced a pawn shop they were waiting for a customer to leave so they could enter, to Ramey.

"What are you smiling about?" he asked her.

* * * * *

The day after the broadcast was business, or lack of, as usual. Clyde didn't open with him and the only people who came inside actually paid money to take things. Next day he didn't have to work until three. That's when he traded shifts with Clyde. (They were the only two employees, and technically Clyde wasn't even that.)

"What are you getting into tonight?" asked Paul.

"The usual."

That meant getting high, reading old comics, and watching conspiracy videos on YouTube that only by the grace of Clyde's FDR Democrat father's late influence didn't fall into scary alt-right doomsday prepper territory. As for Paul, it was an average enough evening at Halsey's Hutch. He mostly just watched Comedy Central. The only interesting thing that happened was that Trooper Woods came in.

"Any word?' Paul asked him.

Woods shook his head. "I just wanted a snack."

"Well, we got snacks."

The state trooper headed down the front aisle, scanning the cakes and pastries and donuts, and caught sight of the comic books below the Little Debbie stand.

"Do you buy these?"

Paul had to turn from the television to see what Woods was talking about. "Not from customers, if that's what you mean. Those are my uncle's."

"I've got a big batch of comics my brother gave me. Death of Superman. They worth anything?"

"Not really."

"Come on." Woods flashed a grin. "It's Death of Superman. Sounds like a pretty big deal to me."

Paul sighed. "It's a long story," he said, "but I don't mind to get into it."

And then he told Trooper Woods all about the comic book industry boom-bust of the 1990s. Woods waited patiently enough until Paul was finished. Then he slid the Swiss Roll that he had placed on the counter three minutes previously a little closer to the cash register.

"Just the cake," Woods said.

* * * * *

After he turned off the open sign and the lights and locked the front door, Paul walked around the side of the now-dark store to where he had parked his pickup truck. He slid his truck key into the keyhole. He was just about to twist it when he heard a crunch of a step on the pavement.

"Don't be scared," Ramey said.

She stood with her hands buried in a black hoodie that was too thick for the weather. She had shorts on over her brown boots. Her hair, unwashed, was pulled back with a scrunchie. She had been waiting for him behind the building. Paul may have yelped when he saw her. "I didn't come to hurt you, Paul." She sounded a bit hoarse and far less playful. "I need your help. Will you help me?"

"You're kidding?"

"Didn't you want to be my friend?"

Paul felt some kind of internal vertigo then. He didn't realize how she could possibly know he had sent her the friend request. He thought he had deleted it in time.

"You put a gun in my face," he said.

Ramey shook her head. "I didn't put a gun in your face. Joe put a gun in your face. He won't do that again."

Paul dared scan the pine trees that lined the edge of the parking lot behind him. He could see a distant porch light on through them.

"Is he here with you?" he asked.

"Joe's gone. Don't worry about him."

Paul blinks. The fat man has a gun. He gets it when they turn around to leave. He puts two in Joe's back. Joe falls into the glass door. He doesn't break it, just thumps against it, sliding down, bleeding.

"Why did you come back here?" asked Paul. His lips, he realized, were very, very chapped.

"Because I need your help."

Paul didn't know what to make of that concept. But he didn't quite believe it. "You should turn yourself in."

"That's just stupid, Paul. I didn't kill anybody. It was Joe. It was all his idea. The stickups, everything."

Paul blinks again. She turns faster than the fat man does and puts one right in his leering red-blooded forehead.

"If you tell them that, they'll take it easy on you."

Ramey tapped her left foot down, hard, almost a stomp. "I been in trouble before," she said. "I know better than that."

A car blew down the highway but the highway was fifty feet behind him, on the other side of the shadows, and a lifetime away.

"I can't help you, Ramey." It felt weird to Paul to say her name as if he really knew her.

"All I need is a ride."

He asked her. He actually asked her. "To where?"

"Buffalo, New York." She said it like it wasn't eight hours away. "I got family there."

"That's a long, long drive." Paul's blood pressure in his ears finally quieted down enough for him to hear the crickets in the hills beyond.

Ramey stepped nearer. "I'll fuck you for it," she said.

"Jesus Christ."

"I'll suck your dick." Her expression wasn't sensual, it was determined and straightforward and it made him both scared and sad.

"It's not like that."

"Oh, come on."

Paul was a pervert, maybe, and he hadn't been laid in nearly two years, but he knew right from wrong. He told her, "I'm not going to be your accomplice. Not for sex. Not for nothing."

"Goddammit, Paul," Ramey barked, yanking an object out of her hoodie pocket. "I was trying to be nice."

It was a pistol. She aimed it at him. "Now you're driving me and you don't get to touch this." She meant her body. Paul felt a wicked déjà vu. "Unlock the passenger door," she told him. "Do it."

He pulled out his key with an abrasive scrape and managed to walk around the front of the truck. He unlocked it.

"Open it."

There was staple gun in the passenger door cubby but that was for his friend's band's flyers. And that would be a very stupid thing to try to pull on her.

"What kind of windows do you have?" she asked him.

"They work."

"Are they automatic or hand crank?"

He had driven that truck for six years but still had to double check. He was thinking straight but straight wasn't fast enough. "Crank," he said.

"Roll them down."

He did.

"Now walk around to your side but don't get in until I tell you to."

Paul stopped himself from telling her he wasn't stupid. Because he was stupid. She wouldn't be here if he wasn't. He wound up staring at her through two sets of windows: driver's side and windshield.

"Now open your door."

He had to unlock it first.

"Stay put," Ramey told him.

She stepped, quick as a mink, around to the open passenger door. She aimed her pistol across the seats at Paul.

"Get in," she told him.

He did. She matched his entrance and shifted how she held the gun so that the barrel was toward his midsection.

"Close your door." She shut hers, too.

"Start the truck." The radio kicked on too loud. Ramey smashed her palm into the knob. "Fuck country music," she said, either snarling or smiling. (Paul couldn't tell in the dark.) "Now take me to the interstate."

"Can I buckle up first?" he asked.

"Maybe we both should." And they did. It could have been cute, the mirroring, with a different prop and a different backstory. "Now go."

Paul put the truck into drive. He swung it around the rear of the store. The faulty air conditioner that stuck out from the back wall dripped condensation into the night. He wrapped the truck up the side of the building and saw the crest of the pavement, beyond which lay the highway. Paul put his foot on the gas. Turning the steering wheel sharp, he slammed both the pedal and the horn. The truck sped off the pavement, rose and fell over a dip, and rushed onto the grass toward his uncle's front yard.

"What the—"

Something popped. Shrapnel pierced his belly. Before he could stop it, or even see it, his truck slammed into his uncle's car. Both airbags blew out. Paul was whipped forward and then yanked back. His foot slipped off the pedal. The truck idled, heaving, hurt. Paul turned his head — that hurt, too — to examine his passenger. She was digging around for something in the floorboard.

"Where the hell is it?" she asked.

Paul managed to get unbuckled. He pulled the handle of his door. Then clambered out onto the driveway. His right knee buckled the minute he put real pressure on it. He fell through the dark air onto tiny gray rocks. Paul breathed fire but not out like a dragon. Rather in like a sick man. He put his right hand to his right side and brought it away bloody. She had shot him. That was what that boom had been. Paul was looking across the gravel below the truck. Ramey's brown punk boots landed on the other side.

He crawled. He dragged himself down the driveway, along the length of the wreck, every crawl a misery. She paralleled him, walking slowly but unsteady. She could have been drunk. Dogs barked up and down the creek. They made it sound like a coyote was prowling. (She was.) Paul reached the edge of the metallic tailgate and looked up beyond the hitch. Ramey stepped out from behind the truck with her pistol pointed at him. Blood ran down her nose.

"I thought you liked me, Paul," she said.

A shotgun blast ruined her chest in a slam of blood. The impact sent her toppling backward onto the gravel. Everything smelled of brimstone. The tips of her boots twitched like a dowsing rod over water. Clyde, wearing a bathrobe stained pink, crouched beside his nephew. He propped himself up with his shotgun. The old man's breath smelled like expensive marijuana and cheap bourbon.

"Where did she get you?" he asked.

"In the stomach."

"The ambulance will be here soon."

Then Clyde stood with an effort, almost unbalanced by the weight of his weapon. He took a few halting steps closer to where Ramey Mears lay.

Paul watched him watch her. His right cheek was pressed into the gravel with an almost pleasant sort of pain. He had been crying since his uncle shot her.

"What the hell, girl," he heard Clyde say.

It didn't take an hour for the sirens to get there that time.

Lee Blevins was born in Morehead, Kentucky. He lives in Lexington. His website houses some Northeastern Kentucky history essays.

byleeblevins.com

A Flash of Red

J.B. Stevens

Previously published by *Story and Grit*

Catching a bullet was a possibility, but he was old and comfortable with dying.

He waited for the sting.

* * * * *

Smitty was tired of moving, so he sat on a mossy pile of bricks and sucked air through flared nostrils. It smelled like rotting vegetation. He flexed his bad knee, the result of a bullet in Kosovo. His best friend died that day. No one remembered the U.S. fought in Kosovo. He was happy for the Iraq vets, they always got a thank you.

The sun was coming up over the Savannah River, everything was silent, and the world was calm. Smitty was in the jungle that used to be Mulberry Grove Plantation. His Walmart Special tan slacks and pale yellow dress shirt were no match for the briars. Sweat made the polyester cling to skin. He'd looked for the fugitive all night. If he could just find the little gangbanger he could get to bed. He had to get the job done. Duty mattered.

Even covered in moss the bricks were hurting his ass and he could feel the damp all over his body. He was still out of breath when he stood. Because he was thin everyone thought he was in shape. They were wrong. His ex-spouse was the cook. Ever since they split Smitty didn't eat enough. Thirty years of unfiltered Lucky Strikes probably didn't help either.

After teasing him for awhile, daylight finally broke. This was Smitty's first time at Mulberry Grove. Around here everyone was familiar with the historical marker announcing Eli Whitney's invention of the cotton gin; but going out to the actual site... he didn't know anyone that had ever bothered to make the trip.

Old shit was all over Savannah, but no one paid attention. They were too busy with their own stuff. Smitty wondered if people still use the old cotton gins. Sometimes the old ways were best.

He walked to his beat-up Ford Crown Victoria. Sand fleas got in his mouth; they were chewy. Some voodoo lady from Pin Point had a bug cure. The guys swore it worked, but he didn't take up with that trash.

He moved past a dead animal. It smelled strongly and he covered his nose. It looked like a mule. He rounded the last bend and the modern world returned. His knock-off Rolex said it was almost time for lunch. He got in the Crown Vic and headed to the meetup spot. Minutes later he pulled into a parking lot.

A group of officers stood idle in the humid air talking about a funeral for a motorcycle cop, heart attack. Smitty got out and lit a Lucky Strike. He rubbed fatigue out of his light eyes, and shook leaves out of cropped grey hair.

Smitty found Deputy Chief Flynn. "Want a cigarette, Boss-Man?"

Flynn never seemed to like Smitty. "Those things'll kill you," Flynn said, and smiled.

Everyone was buzzing about last night. It was the first car chase for a lot of the new guys. A voice came across the radio. "What's the fugitive's alias and what are his priors?" the voice said.

Smitty reached for a piece of paper. Flynn picked up his radio mic and said, "Goes by Sonic."

"Like the fast-food place?" the radio crackled.

"Like the hedgehog," Flynn droned.

Silence, then the radio continued. "Okay. Priors are aggravated assault, domestic violence, moonshining, counterfeiting, and an accusation of homicide. Address is…"

Smitty wrote the address, nodded at Flynn, and went to the Crown Vic. "I'm going to do a drive-by of the girlfriend's. Find the hole, find the pole."

Flynn called after Smitty. But Smitty had already closed the car door.

Driving had always calmed Smitty. He enjoyed the way the old Crown Vic handled. Threadbare seats seemed molded to fit his ass. It was the only one left in service. The motor pool officer wanted to get rid of it.

Smitty pulled over next to Yamacraw Village on the northwest side of Savannah. There was graffiti on the walls and trash on the ground. The fugitive's girlfriend lived there with her aunt.

The residents of Yamacraw know a police car when they see one, but his was so old and beat-up they must have assumed it was an out-of-service auction buy. The car's windows had a dark tint job. No one saw the old man inside. Smitty watched a couple of hand-to-hand drug buys in the yard. How many foot chases and rough arrests had he had done here? Too many to count.

Smitty had probably locked up some of these kids' grandfathers. No one cared. While watching the deals go down his phone rang. It was his Ex.

"Hey," Smitty said.

"My half of the home sale equity check didn't come through," said the Ex, who only heard silence. "You OK, Jim?"

His Ex still looked after him. Smitty smiled. "I'll send it out today."

"Thanks."

"I'm doing OK. I drop my retirement paperwork in the spring."

"That's good. You deserve a break. Do some fishing."

"I'd die from boredom."

"Maybe."

"Look, I got to go. If you need anything, call."

"OK."

Things could've gone better with Eric. If he'd been home earlier and left the job at the office then maybe they would still be together. Eric's new guy, Phil the Pharmacist, seemed solid. His record was clean. But damn, Phil was boring.

A young man that looked like the fugitive strolled past. Smitty thought about jumping out, old-school style, but decided to follow policy; safety first and all that. Reaching for the radio, he contacted Flynn.

"Call me on the cell," Flynn said.

Smitty punched up Flynn's number. "I see the suspect."

"Got it. Hold tight."

Moments later Smitty received a group text message containing a picture of the bandit, a bio sheet, his arrest record, a warrant, and the suspect's location.

Smitty radioed, "I'm staying. Keeping eyes on."

Flynn texted. "Keep off the radio unless it is hot. Keep police business secure as possible. Reporters have frequency scanners." The asshole actually signed his text Deputy Chief Flynn.

Smitty watched the suspect move toward an old purple Cadillac that was more rust then metal, though the rims were wire-spoke, chrome, immaculate, and expensive. He waited for a drug deal, but it never happened. The target was getting in the car. If the suspect hit the road, he was gone.

Smitty responded to the group text. "We've got movement, how far out is the team?"

"Fifteen minutes."

"Moving in to make contact."

"Hold off and wait for backup."

"Negative. Time's up."

The Crown Vic humped the curb and groaned across the grass. Smitty turned on the red and blues, opened the door, took a kneeling position behind the engine block, and drew his .40 caliber Glock 22. The adrenaline helped with the pain in his knees. He loved the rush, looked forward to it every time.

"Put your hands on the headliner of the vehicle. No sudden movements."

The men in the vehicle raised their arms and stared at him hard.

"Driver, with your left hand remove the car keys and place them on the roof. Open the trunk."

Smitty noticed people streaming from buildings.

Cellphones came out. Someone yelled "Worldstar!" Another yelled "Fuck the police!"

Smitty continued. "Driver, with your left hand reach out the window and open your door."

The driver did as instructed.

"Step out of the car. Walk to the front. Keep your hands up and turn away from me." The driver did as he was instructed. "Now! Take your shirt off. If you have any weapons tell me."

"Ain't got shit," the driver hollered.

"Walk backwards toward me."

When the man was fifteen feet from the car Smitty continued. "Get on your knees and interlace your fingers behind your head."

The driver kneeled. Smitty moved. Three feet from the driver he holstered his weapon and started to pull his cuffs.

The gunshot was deafening.

Smitty's hearing distorted like he had cotton stuffed in his ears. Everything in his direct line of sight got brighter and sharper. The edges of his vision blurred. He kicked the kneeling man away. The next volley of incoming shots sounded muffled. Smitty dove to his right and drew his weapon again.

There was a large oak to his front. He shot at the car and sprinted to the tree, diving into a pile of yellow fast-food wrappers. Smitty peeked around the tree. Two shots flew past his head. He fired back until his Glock was empty and the slide locked back.

He pulled out his cell and hit redial. Flynn answered. Smitty yelled, "Taking fire! Get here right-fucking-now!"

A shot hit the bark. Another hit the dirt. He slapped in his spare fifteen-round magazine. He looked around and saw the top of the shooter's head over the Caddy's hood. He focused hard on the front sight, aimed it at the perp's hairline peeking over the hood. He controlled his breathing.

Smitty squeezed. A round fired. The weapon jumped. Time slowed. He felt recoil. The front sight rose and fell. The suspect's head snapped back. A flash of red mist.

Smitty moved right. The bandit was in the dirt. The back of his skull was gone and a red pool was forming. Still, you never know, so he put on cuffs. Smitty secured the pistol next to the body.

It hurt to breathe. His right side was wet. A woman screamed, "He leakin'!"

Sirens filled his ears and everything went black.

Smitty saw a bright white light and hoped he was dead. He heard soft crying. It was Eric. Smitty wondered if he brought Phil the Pharmacist.

"How you doing, babe? Why do you treat yourself like this?"

"What happened?"

"He almost killed you."

"But I got him first."

"No one cared about that criminal. You need to keep yourself safe."

A smile crossed his face and the morphine hit his system. Eric held his hand as Smitty passed out.

J.B. Stevens lives in the Southeastern United States with his wife and daughter.

His writing has been featured in Mystery Tribune, Out of the Gutter, Close To The Bone, Thriller Magazine, Punk Noir Magazine, The Dead Mule School of Southern Literature, Criminal Element, and other publications.

jb-stevens.com
Twitter: @IamJBStevens

The Best Kind of Husband

Michael D. Davis

I was sitting in the corner booth of the only diner in town. The same thing I did every day at this time. Waiting for the other two. Me getting here ten minutes early and them arriving ten minutes late was something that had gone on for more years than I care to admit. We hadn't changed, just gotten older.

As I waited for Beatrix and Helen my mind shot like a bullet back to that Monday in March 1969. I was twenty years old and newly married. Hitched to a man that I once thought made the world turn.

Our house was small and cheap and in the middle of the little town we both grew up in. Back then I didn't work. Not because I couldn't; because he didn't want me to. My husband, Denny-Jay, left every morning to repair the town's cars as I sat in an empty house.

That Monday in March was different than any other Monday because I had news. It was just over six months we'd been married and I'd been to the doctor. That Monday in March I was gonna tell Denny-Jay I was carrying his child.

Five was the time he got off of work and when he got home he'd find me sitting at a fully stocked kitchen table. Just waiting for him. But five came and passed, then six came and passed. It was seven o'clock when he finally got home. Denny-Jay stumbled in through the front door drunk as a skunk. I don't know why I was surprised. He'd done it several times in the last six months.

When he got to the kitchen he saw me and said, "Hey, honey," like it was nothing. Avoiding my icy glare he looked at the table full of now-cold food and said, "This all for you, Wilma? You've been gettin' bigger... hopefully, you don't get as big as your boat-like mother." He thought that was funny. Laughing at his own joke, he found himself a drink.

I stood up from the kitchen table. "How perceptive of you, Denny-Jay. I have been getting bigger."

"Damn right you have."

"Because, Denny-Jay, I'm pregnant... if you would've come home after work instead of going out drinking you would've found out over a lovely chicken dinner." I turned away from him and went to the sink where the pans were soaking.

"What?" he said. "But we...we haven't in a week or so."

"Don't I know it," I said, grabbing a sponge.

"Then whose is it, you whore?"

"What?"

"That's not mine. Whose is it?"

I turned toward him. "There's no other man's it could be."

"Bullshit! We haven't had sex in a week and a half. So, is it that bald bastard's from across the street or was it that you got some trucker from the bar?"

"The only one of us that frequents bars around here is you and getting pregnant isn't like pushing a button and there you are. It takes awhile to tell. Now, go to bed, maybe tomorrow you'll have something nice to say to me."

I turned back to the sink as he threw his beer down. I moved my hands over the wet, heavy skillet not doing anything really, just hoping he'd walk away. He didn't. Before I knew it his arms were wrapped tight around me.

"You whore," he said before grabbing me between my legs. "This here is mine, not even yours." His head rested on my shoulder as he spoke.

Twice before when Denny-Jay was upset and drunk he touched me. One was a grope and a slap;

the other was a shove into the wall. I was truly afraid of him with his head next to mine and his hard hands moving about my body.

I went numb all over, gripping the handle of the skillet with all my might. I don't know if I was thinking too much or not at all, but I then brought the skillet up to his forehead just over my shoulder. He kept leaning on me, but his arms went lax. I turned around and he swayed there with a dazed look on his face. He wasn't bleeding. I gripped him by the shirt so he wouldn't fall, then I brought the skillet up again. The entire left side of his head caved in like an old house. He dropped to the floor. This time there was blood. Plenty of it.

Too tired to hold it any longer, the pan clattered to the floor as it slipped from my hand. I stood there for I don't know how long just looking at his crumpled figure on the floor. When I came to my senses again and started to breathe normally, I made my way to the phone.

I picked up the receiver intending to call the police but thought better of it and replaced it on the cradle. I stood there. Staring at the phone. Trying to think. Its high-pierced ring split the silence like a brick through a glass window. Irrationally I thought it was the police calling. Maybe to ask why I didn't phone about bashing my husband in the head with dirty cookware.

I didn't want to answer it, but it just kept ringing and ringing. I couldn't've told you for how long. So, I plucked it again from the cradle and held it gently to my face.

"Hello," I squeaked out.

"Wilma, good, I was about to hang up thinking you went to bed early or something."

"Oh," I said as I let out my breath, "Beatrix, it's you."

"Of course, who were you expecting to call? Elvis?"

"No, it's just… could you come over?"

"Now?"

"Please, it's kind of an emergency."

"Already leaving," she said right before the connection broke.

It was only a minute before her car pulled up out front. However, I'm sure if you let her tell it she'd say she ran the entire way. Cutting through neighbors' yards, attempting to avoid rabid pet dogs that were chained up in slipshod manners and even leaping a fence in a single bound all to come to the aid of her friend. Although she only lived two blocks over.

I let her in, dodging her questions that were shot off with each step deeper into the house.

When we got to the kitchen, Beatrix took one look at Denny-Jay, clicked her tongue and shook her head in a disappointed manner and said, "Good golly, Wilma you got blood all over perfectly good chicken." Then she looked at me and smiled, which made me smile even though I didn't feel like doing so.

"Alright, I'll call Don and tell him I won't be home for awhile as you take my damn jacket."

A few minutes later we were back in the kitchen looking down at my husband.

"That old trunk in the living room. Is it empty? Wilma?"

"Oh, uh…mostly. It just has old clothes in it."

"Well, dump it out and get it in here."

I did as I was told as quick as I could. It was a big trunk and rather old but lightweight. She told me to change and we threw my bloody dress into the trunk first. Then Denny-Jay. It took us both to pretzel him into the box. It was to our luck that he was rail thin; his height, on the other hand, made for a problem. I then took this cracked bowl I'd been meaning to pitch out and collected the little bits of Denny-Jay and his skull that had scattered across the linoleum. I put the bowl in his hands and shut the trunk.

"Wait," said Beatrix.

"What?"

"Let's stuff the skillet in there too."

"But that's my best one."

"Are you really gonna use it again?"

"But…but it's cast iron."

"Wilma, it is a murder weapon."

"Fine," I said, opening the trunk again while mumbling to myself some not-so-nice words. After we shoved my best skillet in with my dead husband, Beatrix sent me out to see how dark it had gotten. It wasn't pitch black but the sun was down.

Beatrix was by far the strongest woman I've ever known. She was short and wide and when she said it was dark enough out, she picked up that trunk like it was a box full of pillows. I opened the door for her and then the trunk of her car. It was a beat-up '55 Oldsmobile and after we closed the back end we were off.

All three of us.

We headed north out of town. It wasn't long before the pavement turned to gravel. I didn't know where we were going, but Beatrix seemed to have things all figured out. I leaned my head against the window and closed my eyes. The next time I opened them, we were stopped.

It was a little farm. An old barn with an old house and an old car sitting between the two. I'd never been there before. But I knew where I was. It was Helen Messer's farm. I knew her through Beatrix and often saw her at church. It made sense to come here.

I spoke to Helen once and she said, "I have the best husband of them all."

I didn't respond because I'd heard she was a widow. She continued, saying, "I married a man who wasn't mean but just there taking up space and only two months after our wedding he dropped dead of a stroke leaving me with a great little farm."

Beatrix was already on the porch when I awoke. I got out to join them. Helen was different in appearance than Beatrix in almost every way. She was tall and wire lean, with long blonde straw-like hair, and a tanned, pinched face that seemed to center around a forever lit cigarette.

"Hi, Helen," I said, walking up on the porch.

"Hello, Wilma," she said, talking around her cigarette. "I hear you got a husband to throw away."

I reddened with embarrassment at her frankness but she seemed not to judge or, in fact, be bothered at all.

"I don't know what came over me," I said. "It was like I was sleepwalking."

"Honey, I don't care," she said.

Beatrix put her hand on my back and said, "It's alright. We knew Denny-Jay and even if we didn't I'm sure we'd still understand."

"Bea, I wish I'd picked a good one like yours."

"Don may not have a temper and he may not drink, but he has his faults like every man."

Helen snorted and said, "The best kind of husband is a dead husband."

The conversation seemed to come to a stop after that. There was a small strip of land in one of Helen's fields made up of trees and other brush. She'd used her tractor to pull out a stump of an old dead tree located there not but a few days prior. The dirt was soft and loose and ready.

We loaded the trunk into the bed of Helen's old truck behind the barn. Threw in some shovels as well. I asked about the noise of the truck, wondering if someone might hear and get suspicious. Helen said not to worry, that her nearest neighbors were two miles back the way we came.

The hole where the stump had been was wide but not particularly deep. It took some doing but we finally made the trunk fit. Once it was in the ground and covered, the three of us just stood there looking at it.

"People," I said, "usually say things at times like this but I don't feel inclined. I'm just grateful for you two."

"Don't worry about it," Beatrix said.

"Son of a bitch shouldn't be found till long after we're all dead. If he's ever found," Helen said.

We went home and I spent the night cleaning the kitchen and throwing away the chicken. Some months after that night my first daughter was born. She was a beautiful baby and the best thing to come from Denny-Jay.

Me and Denny-Jay were a lovely topic of conversation in a small town where people talk more than they do anything else. I was worried that as people chewed on and guessed at things that sooner or later someone's hammer would hit the nail. But it never happened. The theory that everyone took to heart was that when I told Denny-Jay I was with child he just walked out. It was supported by the widely known fact that six months into our marriage he'd already stepped out on me. A few times.

From our usual corner booth, I had a clear view of the entrance. Beatrix was coming in the door followed by Helen when a young man tried to push around them. Beatrix gave him an elbow which threw him against the wall.

"Damn, old lady," the boy bellered.

Beatrix continued walking and said, "Watch who you try to push around, you ill-mannered sack of shit. I buried men bigger than you."

Michael D. Davis was born and raised in a small town in Iowa. A high school graduate and avid reader, he has aspired to be a writer for years. He's written over fifty short stories, ranging in genre from comedy to horror and flash fiction to novella, some of which have been published in Yellow Mama webzine, Out of the Gutter Online, Near to the Knuckle online magazine, Horla, and Sirens Call.

He continues in his accursed pursuit of a career in the written word and, in his hunt, Michael's love for stories in all genres and mediums will not falter.

Malcolm Lost His Head

John Kojak

Malcolm lost his head again, Terry thought when he found Windex, the family's scruffy grey tabby who liked to lick dusty windows, crudely skinned and hanging by a shoelace from a tree. Terry took out the small buck knife he kept in his pocket, cut the cat down, then carried Windex's lifeless body over to a nearby rabbit hole and kicked dirt and leaves over the opening until he was sure no one else would find her.

Just like he had done with the other dead animals, rabbits and squirrels mostly, that he found mutilated in the stand of trees behind his family's small farmhouse.

When Terry returned home, his younger brother Malcolm was sitting on the front porch playing with the cat's favorite toy, a long piece of yellow ribbon their mother had tied to the end of a hickory switch. He looked innocent enough, with his chubby round face and curly blond locks, but his muddy jeans were speckled with drops of dark, dried blood — and one of his shoelaces was missing.

"Hey, Terry," Malcolm said. He flicked the ribbon out onto the deck, and then pulled it back slowly in a long s-curved pattern. The same way he did when he was playing with the cat. "Have you seen Windex?"

Terry looked into Malcolm's eyes. They were not the eyes of a twelve-year-old. Dark shadows danced behind their pale blue facade. "Windex is dead, Malcolm," Terry replied sullenly. "I found her body out in the woods near the creek. It...it looked like a coyote may have got to her."

Terry didn't know why he lied. He knew the truth, and so did Malcolm. But Malcolm was Terry's little brother, and his mother made Terry promise that he would always protect Malcolm — even from himself.

"Windex is dead?" Malcolm jumped up, his eyes filling with big crocodile tears. "No, not Windex!" he yelled, then stamped his feet before running into the house.

Malcolm was good, but Terry had seen his act before. The first time was two years ago after he found Oreo, the black and white spotted rabbit Malcolm had been given for his tenth birthday, stomped to death in the field behind the garden. Oreo's body was as flat as a sheet. Every bone in the rabbit's body had been broken, pulverized, and its innards splayed out underneath like it had been run over by a large truck. But it wasn't a truck. It was Malcolm. Terry knew it as sure as he knew his own name.

Terry didn't want his little brother to get in trouble, so he told his parents that he found Oreo's trampled body by the side of the road. Malcolm cried that night too, but Terry could see the dark flames flickering behind Malcolm's teary eyes. That was the first time.

It wouldn't be the last.

In the beginning Terry believed the killings would pass. That they were just the result of a child's natural curiosity with death, but it didn't take long to see that it was cruelty, not curiosity, driving Malcolm to kill. All the dead animals Terry found died a horrible death, each more grotesque and torturous than the last. Some had their eyes gouged out, or their tongues crudely cut off. Others had been burned alive. The only constant was they had all suffered.

Terry lied again when he told his parents about Windex. He said a coyote killed her. His father seemed relieved; he had never taken to the cat like his mother had. She was genuinely sad when he told her Windex was dead, and it hurt him to lie to his mother. He thought about telling her the truth, that it was Malcolm, and about how the cat had been skinned alive and hung on a branch to die by her favorite son, the precious blond angel who could do no wrong in her eyes.

But she wouldn't believe it. "Malcolm? That boy wouldn't harm a fly," she would've said. She didn't see the shadows dancing behind his eyes. No one else did. Like it or not, Terry thought, Malcolm's secrets were his now as well. It would be up to him to watch over Malcolm, to protect him.

He would have to be his brother's keeper.

Terry was relieved when the last few weeks of summer ended without further incident and it was time to go back to school. The long walks to the schoolhouse gave the brothers a chance to talk. It was the only time Terry felt Malcolm was still truly himself.

The first morning they walked in silence for several minutes before Malcolm turned to Terry and asked, "Do you still love me?"

"Of course I do. You're my little brother."

"But what about Windex?"

Terry was surprised; Malcolm had never discussed any of the animals before.

"What about her?"

"You know…" Malcolm asked coyly, seeming to relish playing his part in their little game.

"I just...I don't want you to do that anymore. Okay?"

"Okay, Terry. I was just trying to help her, that's all."

"Help her? I don't see how anything needs that kind of help, Malcolm."

"Sometimes...sometimes they do."

"Well, don't ever try to help me. How's that?"

"I wouldn't, Terry. I just wouldn't."

Terry wanted to believe him — but was anybody really safe?

Terry liked school. The schoolhouse was a small three-room building that separated the children based on age. Although they were not in the same classroom, Terry felt that he could keep a much better eye on Malcolm while they were in school than he could on their farm. The new school year was just as routine and boring as the last, and that was fine with Terry. He needed a break from Malcolm's madness, and after a few blissfully uneventful weeks Terry was beginning to forget about the horrors he had discovered that summer. But then something happened, something that had never happened before — a girl took an interest in Malcolm. Not in a romantic or playful way though; she was mean. She teased him and said he was dumber than he looked, and that he looked pretty damn dumb. Mean.

Her name was Mary Jo Simpson, a lanky redhead with big feet and a tongue like a rattlesnake. Terry warned her. He told her to leave Malcolm alone. But she kept at it, pulling on his curly blond hair and calling him stupid. Terry thought Malcolm would belt her in the mouth, or hit her over the head with a stick, but to his surprise he never retaliated. It went on for a whole week, and nothing. Terry wasn't sure whether to be worried or relieved. But he was scared out of his boots when Mary Jo didn't show up to school on Monday morning.

She was missing for three days before they found her body buried under a stack of rocks near the quarry. Her head had been smashed with a large piece of limestone, and someone had done things to that girl that no one, at least no one in a small town in West Texas, had ever heard of, much less seen. Terry knew there was only one person that cruel. He knew it was Malcolm.

Terry thought about telling his parents — someone, anyone! — about Malcolm, but a few hours after her body was found the sheriff arrested a couple of hobos who had been hopping trains nearby. Most folks had no problem believing they had killed Mary Jo. After all, they couldn't believe that anyone from their little town would do those things.

They just were not those kind of people.

Terry laid awake in bed the night after Mary Jo's funeral. He was wracked with guilt about what happened, what he had allowed to happen, to that girl. He couldn't sleep, but he wasn't the only one. He could hear the muffled sounds of his parents' voices downstairs. Curious, he got out of bed and made his way silently down the stairs, stopping halfway to listen.

"There is no way Malcolm had anything to do with what happened to that poor girl," his mother said.

"I ain't sayin' that. But there is something wrong with that boy, you have to know that," his father replied in a hushed but urgent tone.

"He's just a child."

"A child that likes to cut the feet off of chickens—"

"You don't know he did that. You didn't see him do it."

"There was blood on the boy's clothes and they was covered in feathers!"

Terry listened in stunned silence as his mother began to weep. He thought he was the only one who knew about Malcolm.

"Maybe we should take him up to San Angelo to see a doctor," his mother said, choking back tears.

"I'm gonna talk to the boy in the morning. Find out what's going on inside that head of his. Then we'll decide."

The hair on the back of Terry's neck stood up as he felt the presence of someone on the staircase behind him.

"What's going on? Why is Momma crying?" Malcolm whispered.

"She's sad about Mary Jo, that's all." Terry grabbed Malcolm's arm and rushed him back up the stairs. "Come on, let's get back to bed."

Terry led Malcolm back to his room and tucked him into his bed. As he looked down at his little brother it was hard for him to believe the chubby, angelic face staring back at him was capable of such evil.

"Are you sure they weren't talking about me, Terry?"

"Of course not. Now go to sleep," Terry said as he kissed his brother goodnight. "Everything is going to be alright." Terry lied. He knew if their parents were getting suspicious…well, it was just a matter of time before they learned the truth.

"Do you still love me?"

Terry's mind flashed back to the image of Windex's bloody body swinging from the tree, poor Oreo, and now, Mary Jo. Cats and rabbits were one thing; little girls were another. "Of course I do…but you weren't supposed to do it no more. You promised."

"I know I did," Malcolm said with some remorse, then the flame came back in his eye. "But she was mean to me. She said I was stupid. She pulled my hair."

"People are going to say and do a lot worse than that, Malcolm. Believe me. But you can't keep…helping them."

"But what if they want me to? What if they're asking for it?"

"The whole world is asking for it. What are you going to do? Help them all?"

"I don't know," Malcolm whined, then — flames. "Sounds kinda nice, though."

"You got lucky this time. They're going to send them two hobos up to see Old Sparky for what you done. One day it's gonna be you…and then what?"

"You wouldn't tell, would you?"

"No, I-I reckon I wouldn't…but everything's not up to me."

The next morning Terry woke Malcolm up early and tried to get him out of the house before his parents got up. He knew something was coming, but he wanted one more day with what was left of his little brother before it did. They snuck out the back door a little before dawn, grabbed a couple of fishing poles out of the small wooden shed behind the house, and were on their way down to the creek when they heard their father's voice boom from the back steps, "Malcolm, get back here. I need to talk to you."

Terry and Malcolm froze in the early morning shadows.

"Wha-what does he want to talk to me for, Terry?"

Terry was tired of lying. "I think he might have found something…a chicken maybe."

A jagged smile cracked across Malcolm's face. "It was a cockerel."

Their father walked up, put his arm around Malcolm's shoulders. "Terry, go on now. I have to talk to your brother."

Terry looked back over his shoulder as they walked away. Their dad might have found a dead chicken, but Terry didn't think he knew how crazy Malcolm truly was. Terry thought about running back to the house and telling his parents about Mary Jo and the animals that Malcolm had killed. They might believe it now, they might...

But he didn't go back.

Instead, he walked down to the creek, stuck his pole in the mud, and waited. He watched as the sun climbed higher and higher into the baked blue West Texas sky. When the sun was directly overhead, he figured he'd waited long enough. If Malcolm hadn't come, it was because it was over. He didn't know what would happen now, but he felt a huge sense of relief as grabbed his pole and started making his way back to the house.

As he walked through the dense brush he began to smell the acrid odor of smoke wafting through the mesquite trees. The sense of relief turned to trepidation. He increased his pace, darting through the trees until he hit an open field and could see a dark column of smoke rising from the direction of their house. He dropped his pole and broke into a full sprint.

When he crested the hill in back of their farmhouse he could see their home completely engulfed in flames. He ran toward the fire, but the heat was so intense he had to stop and shield himself beside the shed. That is when he noticed something else — someone walking through the shimmering waves of heat.

It was Malcolm.

"What happened? Where are mom and dad?" Terry shouted.

Malcolm's golden yellow hair was smoldering and his hands were covered with blisters. "They didn't want me no more. They were going to send me away."

"What are you talking about?"

"They wanted me to go see a psy-psy—"

"A psychiatrist?"

"Yeah, one of those..."

"They just want you to get better, Malcolm."

"But then I wouldn't be able to help things no more. I like helping things." Malcolm giggled like a macabre little schoolgirl.

"What did you do? Where are they?"

"Momma was crying — so I helped her. Daddy didn't want me to, but I did. I helped them both."

Terry doubled over in shock and pain when he realized his parents were dead. He looked up into the flames. He should have said something in the beginning, when it was just squirrels and rabbits. His parents might have been able to stop Malcolm, or at least get him help. But it was too late for that now. Malcolm had completely lost his head. He wouldn't stop killing and Terry couldn't hide the truth much longer, even if he wanted to. It was just a matter of time until Malcolm got caught, then he would spend the rest of his life in prison or, worse, end up sitting in Old Sparky one day, just like them hobos. Terry couldn't allow that to happen.

Not to his little brother.

Malcolm turned back toward the burning house. "What's going to happen now? Do you think they'll send us to live with Aunt Sharon in the city? I like the city...lots of things need help in the city."

"I don't know, Malcolm." Terry turned to his brother. "You done some bad things."

"You still love me, don't you?"

"Of course I do. You're my little brother."

Malcolm smiled and turned back to watch the flames and smoke. As long as his brother still loved him, he believed everything would be alright.

Terry opened the door to the shed, reached in, and grabbed the hickory-handled axe their father used to chop wood. "But I promised Momma I would protect you...even from yourself," he said before swinging the axe across his body in a wide sweeping arc that took Malcolm's head off with a single cut of its blade. A powerful jet of blood sprayed out of Malcolm's neck as his body collapsed to the ground like a bloody bag of bricks. Malcolm's head cartwheeled wildly through the air for several seconds before landing eyes up at Terry's feet. The light was gone from Malcolm's eyes, but the shadows were still there.

Terry knew he could never have his family back, but at least they could all be together, he thought. He bent down and lifted his little brother's lifeless body onto his shoulder with one arm and then grabbed Malcolm's severed head by its burnt and bloody blond locks with the other. He walked toward the raging flames until he was standing on the burning porch surrounded by the blazing inferno. As the fire licked at his flesh, Terry tossed Malcolm's head through the shattered doorway, and then heaved his brother's body into the burning house behind it. The flames would have consumed Terry as well, but a massive fireball suddenly erupted and blew him off the porch and into the yard.

When the fire department arrived they found Terry's blackened body lying on the grass in front of the smoldering ruins of the farmhouse. He was badly burned, going in and out of consciousness, but still alive.

"What happened here, son?" a firemen asked.

Terry's eyes cracked open and he whispered, "Malcolm lost his head."

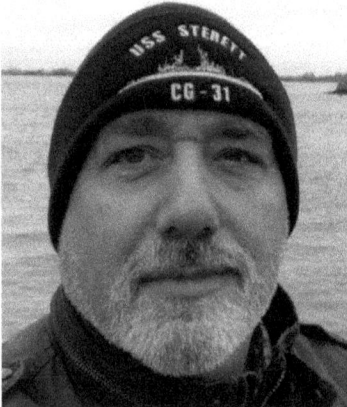

John Kojak is a graduate of The University of Texas and a Navy veteran who now lives and writes in the foothills of Northern California. His short stories and poetry have appeared in numerous publications, including most recently in Pulp Modern, Switchblade, Serial Magazine, The American Journal of Poetry, Harbinger Asylum, and California's Best Emerging Poets 2019.

Twitter: @John Kojak

OTHER BOOKS FROM
BLUE ROOM BOOKS

I AM ISRAEL — Lions and Lambs of the Land

(2018)

Jedwin Smith

Rock Around The Block

(2019)

Alan White

Prose and Cons:

Advice from a Music Legend

who's seen it all: Question Everything

Len Barry

(Coming 2020/2021)

STORIES OF SOUTHERN HUMOR and CRIME: ANTHOLOGY

Southern Crime
Southern Humor
— ANTHOLOGIES —
BlueRoomBooks.com
Decatur, Georgia

[384]

www.ingramcontent.com/pod-product-compliance
Lightning Source LLC
Chambersburg PA
CBHW050449270326
41927CB00009B/1671